Children with Emotional and Behavioural Difficulties and Communication Problems

There is always a reason

Melanie Cross

Jessica Kingsley Publishers
London and New York

First published in the United Kingdom in 2004
by Jessica Kingsley Publishers Ltd
116 Pentonville Road
London N1 9JB, England
and
29 West 35th Street, 10th fl.
New York, NY 10001-2299, USA

www.jkp.com

Copyright © Melanie Cross 2004

Library of Congress Cataloging in Publication Data
A CIP catalog record for this book is available from the Library of Congress

British Library Cataloguing in Publication Data
A CIP catalogue record for this book is available from the British Library

ISBN 1 84310 135 1

Printed and Bound in Great Britain by
Athenaeum Press, Gateshead, Tyne and Wear

Contents

List of Tables

Acknowledgements

In writing this book I felt as if I experienced a wide range of communication, emotional and behavioural difficulties. The book is therefore dedicated to all those who helped me through those difficult times. First, it is dedicated to the wonderful Cross boys, Steve, Jim and Adam, for being patient and supportive. Second, thanks go to the Gilson girls and boys: Jools for her proof reading and encouraging comments; Angie, Peggy and John for listening to me and being sympathetic. Thanks are also due to Angela Sloan for her support and impressive professionalism. I also want to dedicate this to everyone at ISP, young people and adults alike, for everything they have taught me. Grateful thanks are also due to all those kind people who helped me by reading drafts and giving feedback. And finally it is also dedicated to those who have far more difficult times than I can imagine; I hope this book can be a step towards making things better.

Introduction

This is the book I needed when I began to work with children and young people with emotional and behavioural difficulties (EBD). As a speech and language therapist I knew about communication but I found it difficult to understand how communication problems related to EBD; was there a link between the two and if so, why? Initially I had difficulty persuading other professionals that communication problems were significant for these young people; after all, many of them had had severely disrupted lives and little formal education, so did a few additional speech and language problems really matter? The short answer and the main thrust of this book is that, yes, they do matter. They matter because emotional and language development are linked and intertwined. Communication problems can impair someone's ability to interact, manage their behaviour, learn and think.

My initial impressions of working with children with EBD were mixed. I was horrified one morning by the sight of a nine-year-old having a violent 'temper tantrum' like a two-year-old. He was expressing rage beyond anything I had ever experienced and he appeared to be totally out of control. Of course, it wasn't really what had happened in the playground which had caused this reaction but something grim in his past, but that wasn't immediately obvious. I was impressed by the adults with him who managed to gently 'sandwich' him between them on a bench until he was able to calm down. They could see beyond the appalling behaviour to the terrified child. They didn't want to punish him but to help him understand that he was safe and that they didn't want him to get hurt. As I got to know this boy I found out that he had specific communication problems which meant that, although he was bright, he was not able to say what he wanted to very easily and he did not always understand what others said to him.

These communication problems had not been identified before, even though they were often the cause of great frustration for him. This communication frustration was an additional load on a young man who was already struggling with coming to terms with his past, who was unable to make friends and who was not progressing in school. Indeed, I shall argue that his communication problems and those of so many like him directly affected his ability to learn, reason and interact with others. Language and communication skills are central to us as people and, where there are communication problems, young people have great difficulty achieving their potential.

Much of this book is also about seeing beyond the behaviour, because there is always a reason, and dealing with the reasons why will change the behaviour. This book aims to enable anyone working with children and young people who have emotional and behavioural problems to be aware of potential communication difficulties, to recognise some and to have some understanding of how they could respond to them in an enabling way.

There is evidence for a strong link between emotional and language development. Since emotional and communication difficulties often coexist, Chapter 1 begins with a review of theories about how the two develop typically and how they might be linked. As regards language acquisition, the relative importance of factors within the child and within his or her environment is discussed. Although there are various theories of language development, most stress the importance of interaction with a significant person who helps the infant express his or her needs and feelings. Even though the impetus to communicate may be innate, children will not learn to interact verbally if there is no one who is able to interact with them responsively.

Attachment theory also describes how a reciprocal relationship with a significant adult is important for emotional development. Securely attached children use more complex language than maltreated children. Therefore, a sensitive and contingent relationship between child and carer seems to be important for both emotional and communication development. Indeed, language and emotional development are intertwined along with the development of thinking skills.

Given that emotional and language development are probably linked, is it also the case that disruptions in either can affect the other? Chapter 2 considers the literature on the co-occurrence of psychopathology and communication difficulties. Epidemiological studies confirm that there is a strong association between the two. It is likely that the relationship between these two is complex, as there are several possible theoretical links between language impairment and emotional and behavioural problems, with evidence to support each link. There is good evidence to suggest that communication difficulties can lead on to emotional, behavioural and psychiatric problems. Difficulties in understanding language seems to be a high risk factor for the development of psychiatric problems, but expressive difficulties also seem to be responsible for some behavioural problems. The mechanism for communication difficulties resulting in emotional and behavioural problems could be through impaired interactions and/or cognitive deficits, such as limited verbal mediation that impairs behavioural regulation.

There is less evidence for emotional and behavioural problems being the cause of communication difficulties, and this is discussed. Selective mutism, where a young person is only able to communicate in some situations, is a possible candidate for a psychiatric difficulty being the cause of communication problems, but the evidence for this is equivocal. Autism and schizophrenia are 'psychiatric' conditions where communication deficits are part of the diagnosis, but it is unclear whether they cause communication problems or whether communication difficulties are simply an integral part of these conditions. In either case, it is unlikely that these account for much of the association between emotional and behavioural difficulties and communication difficulties. Attention Deficit Hyperactivity Disorder (ADHD) is very closely associated with communication difficulties, especially in children who have problems with the social use of language. It may be that some kinds of communication difficulties and ADHD are both due to executive function deficits; that is, deficiencies in the cognitive skills necessary for self-regulation, which include the development of 'private speech'. Again, although there is a close association between communication difficulties and ADHD, there is insufficient evidence to say that ADHD 'causes' communication problems.

There are many factors which could lead to both emotional and behavioural difficulties and communication problems, and these are considered in detail. Adverse environmental factors, such as perinatal complications, psychosocial stress and low socio-economic status, can affect language and emotional development. Interaction and in particular, attachment difficulties, also seem to be implicated in atypical emotional and language development. The effects of child abuse also appear to be devastating to both emotional and language development, but it is not always clear whether the abuse or the developmental impairments come first. The rate of language development seems to be related to the time spent in neutral affect, so children who are abused or neglected are very likely to have impaired language development. Language development can also affect emotional development because language is necessary to describe and regulate emotions and is therefore an important part of emotional intelligence. Learning difficulties can lead to both emotional and communication problems. However, they cannot entirely explain the association between the two, since not all children with emotional and behavioural problems and communication difficulties have learning problems as well. This chapter concludes that the causation of emotional, behavioural and language difficulties is likely to be multifactorial. The consequences of such complex causation are that many children suffer manifold emotional, behavioural and learning difficulties which need to be addressed with reference to each other.

Although there are strong links between language and emotional development, there is a body of literature deriving from work in child psychiatry which suggests that there may be large numbers of children with emotional and behavioural problems who have unsuspected speech and language difficulties. Chapter 3 considers the significance of this research. In order to do this it is important to know the prevalence of communication difficulties in the general population. However, this is not a simple matter, since there are various definitions of language impairment used in prevalence studies. It seems that approximately 6 per cent of the general child population have communication difficulties. Identifying and charting the natural history of communication problems is further complicated because, although there seems to be a decline in communication difficulties as children reach school age, there is also evidence for some difficulties persisting into adolescence, and we cannot be sure which of these are likely to persist. Communication problems also seem to change in nature over time. Nonetheless, the prevalence of communication difficulties in the 'normal' population is much lower than that in children with emotional and behavioural problems. The literature suggests that perhaps two thirds of the child psychiatric population in both North America and the UK have communication difficulties, with many of these problems remaining undetected. This finding has been replicated in schools for children with emotional and behavioural problems, where the prevalence of undetected communication problems seems to be very high.

The significance of such undetected communication difficulties is discussed in terms of their negative impact on behaviour, emotional development, educational progress and social interactions. The main effect of communication difficulties for a child or young person is an increase in anxiety and frustration, which can manifest itself in unacceptable behaviour. Language impairments have also been shown to have a devastating effect on the development of literacy skills and this can further add to frustration and lowered self-esteem. If, as is often the case, a child or young person's communication difficulties affect his or her social use of language, this has a deleterious effect on social interactions and social problem-solving, which can further exacerbate emotional and behavioural problems.

Children with previously undetected communication problems are also at risk of being misunderstood, their inappropriate responses being seen as a lack of compliance rather than a lack of understanding. Children and young people with undetected communication problems may also be subjected to inappropriate, verbally based interventions. While a child's communication problems remain undetected, their behaviour may be misinterpreted as lack of co-operation or defiance. It is possible that identifying communication problems in this population and treating them could reduce emotional and behavioural problems as well as social and educational difficulties.

It is also important to think about why communication problems are undetected in this population. It may be that those affected have more salient emotional and behavioural difficulties. There is also evidence that unidentified communication problems may be relatively subtle. Parents of children with undetected communication problems may themselves be disadvantaged and therefore not in a good position to identify difficulties in their children. A further complication is that language impairments can change in nature over time, making them more difficult to identify.

The main reason why communication difficulties remain undetected is that there is a general lack of awareness and training about such problems and their potential negative effects. Therefore, professionals who work with children and young people who have emotional and behavioural difficulties may not be looking for communication difficulties, and consequently they are not found.

Chapter 4 concentrates on children in public care and how the research on problems with language and emotional development relates to them. These are children and young people who often have greater needs in terms of education and health care than their peers, as well as greater difficulty accessing the services they need. Although attempts are being made to rectify the situation, they still tend to fail educationally and have poor health.

There is evidence that their special educational needs may not always be recognised and met, and that services may be unavailable to help with their complex learning and emotional difficulties. Services for children with emotional and behavioural problems are not uniformly available throughout the UK. This means that many children have to move from their locality or forgo the special educational help they need. It may be that unidentified communication problems are just one type of undetected special need, which contributes to the learning and social adjustment difficulties of children 'looked after' by the local authority.

Children and young people in public care also have greater health needs than other children, and evidence is reviewed which shows that these health needs may not be met. There is a high incidence of psychopathology in children in 'out-of-home' placements. In addition, there is a high incidence of chronic illness and developmental delays, as well as behaviour problems. There is also some evidence that potentially treatable psychiatric problems are missed and that other health needs may go unmet. These children may also be 'at risk' through missing out on medical screening programmes. Therefore, it is not surprising that communication problems also go undetected in this population.

One reason why children 'looked after' by the local authority may not have their health and educational needs met is that the various professionals working with them have differing expectations of themselves and each other in relation to these children. Current initiatives, such as *Quality Protects*, are seeking to address this, but teachers, social workers, medical professionals and foster carers all see themselves as having separate responsibilities, and therefore it is not always easy to co-ordinate services. This is particularly the case where the professionals are employed by, and work in, totally separate systems of care. For example, there is an ongoing debate about whether speech and language therapy for school-aged children should be funded by health or education. Meeting the needs of 'looked after' children is further complicated by difficulty keeping track of children and their individual needs through changes of foster carer, school and social worker.

Chapter 5 considers the practical problems involved in the identification and assessment of communication difficulties. It is important to identify communication problems because of their negative and potentially long-term effects on thinking, learning and interaction. However, there is no consensus about how to do this. Since language impairments are heterogeneous in nature and any or all areas of language function can be affected, a variety of assessments is necessary to gain a clear picture of the nature of any impairment.

Assessment is further complicated by the various definitions of language impairment; I consider the relevance of these to children with emotional and behavioural difficulties. Another possible confounding factor is that we do not have full knowledge of normal language development, so identifying deviations from the norm is problematic. This chapter goes on to discuss the advantages and disadvantages of standardised formal assessments including comparisons of the usefulness of standardised tests and informal assessments.

Informal assessments are important since problems with the social use of language seem to be particularly prevalent amongst children with emotional and behavioural difficulties, and such problems are probably best assessed by informal methods. The evidence for specific deficits, which could be 'markers' of language impairment because they are commonly found in language-impaired children, is reviewed. Two of these are sound processing difficulties and problems with narrative structure.

The contribution to assessment by the child or young person themselves and others who know them is invaluable, and ways of collecting this type of information are discussed. It is also important to be sensitive to the ways in which children and young people with emotional and behavioural problems might respond to formal and informal assessment. Lack of co-operation or eagerness to please could both influence the results. It is crucial to consider how a young person with a previously undetected communication problem might feel about assessment. Some are relieved because they knew there was 'something going on' but did not know what. Others feel that they are 'just stupid', so sensitive explanations of the nature of communication problems are necessary. Some are acutely self-conscious and embarrassed about their 'problems' and not willing to own them. We can't force an assessment or a diagnosis on them.

Information gathered from those who know a child or young person well is therefore very important. There are various ways that non-speech and language therapists can collect evidence which might help identify communication difficulties. There is evidence that even just the recognition of a communication problem can improve interactions because it can alter expectations; this is an example of how knowledge can promote understanding.

Chapter 6 is practically based. There are many proven programmes and strategies available and, although there is still much research to be done to find which interventions are most effective, there is a lot that can be done to help young people with emotional, behavioural and communication difficulties.

There are broad strategies available, the most important of which are prevention and early intervention. Initiatives such as *Sure Start* are aiming to support families where the children might be at risk of developing emotional, behavioural and communication difficulties. The other broad strategies discussed in this chapter are available to anyone working with a young person who has communication, emotional and behavioural difficulties, and include developing a positive and supportive relationship. Communicating and learning about emotions happens through interacting with others, so the importance of a relationship where young people are supported in their learning should not be underestimated. Specific strategies which will enable interaction with a child or young person who has communication difficulties are also discussed. Given that this book is about young people who often face multiple difficulties, many professionals will need to collaborate with each other and with the young person and their family in order to work towards a positive outcome. 'Joined-up working' has become something of a cliché but that shouldn't detract from its importance; it is another important tool in helping young people overcome complex difficulties. Anyone working with a young person with emotional and behavioural difficulties may be faced with dilemmas about how to respond to inappropriate behaviour (anyone with children also considers this on a daily basis). There are no easy answers, but there are some useful questions to ponder in this section of the chapter with regard to enabling appropriate behaviour. Perhaps the most important broad strategy which needs to be implemented is developing training opportunities for those working with young people with emotional, behavioural and communication difficulties, as little is available at present.

There are skills and attributes which children and young people with communication and emotional/behavioural difficulties would benefit from acquiring, such as emotional intelligence, good self-esteem, play skills, learning how to make friends, social problem-solving and narrative skills. Anyone working with young people with complex difficulties can help them develop these important skills, and in this part of the chapter I discuss ways to teach them.

Children and young people who have complex problems may also need specific interventions in order to achieve their potential. Some of these are discussed, although, as with the rest of the chapter, it is impossible to include all available options. Specific interventions in school, speech and language therapy and psychotherapy are discussed.

The conclusions of this book include a call for more research, but there is a lot that can be done given the current state of knowledge:

- Children and young people with emotional and behavioural difficulties should be screened for communication difficulties, because they are very likely to occur and have negative effects on their social, emotional and educational development.

- Speech and language therapy should be available for children with emotional and behavioural difficulties.

- Joined-up working is vital to help young people who have emotional, behavioural and communication difficulties achieve their potential.

CHAPTER 1

Are Language and Emotional Development Linked?

Perhaps the most important message in this book is that young people who have emotional and behavioural problems are also very likely to have communication difficulties (Benasich, Curtiss and Tallal 1993), and more worryingly these communication problems have often gone unrecognised (Cohen *et al.* 1998b). It is also the case that young people who have language impairments often develop emotional and behavioural difficulties as they get older. In order to try to understand why there seems to be this link between emotional and language difficulties, we need to consider how emotional and language development usually occur. Theories and research about the typical development of communication and language not only give us insight into how problems might occur but they can also provide us with ideas about how we might be able to help young people with communication and emotional difficulties.

What are language and communication skills?

Before considering how language develops it is necessary to define the component skills necessary for communication. Communication is a complex process, but we tend not to notice its intricacy, as for most of us 'it just happens', rapidly and without conscious thought. Language is also easy to take for granted, because it is everywhere: we use language to talk about and organise our experiences; in order to build relationships; to learn about the world, and ourselves; and to think and imagine. There are, of course, many types of language: spoken, written, symbol-based or signed. It is also important not to forget that language is just one communication tool; others include non-verbal features such as intonation and facial expression.

The skills necessary for communication can be divided into form, content and use. In any conversation we use our *understanding* of the form, content and use to interpret what others say and in order to *express* ourselves.

Form

The form of any communication system is basically its structure, and to be an effective communicator you need to be able to *use* and *understand* form effectively. Some of the component skills necessary for this are detailed in Table 1.1. In spoken language this includes the way sounds are ordered to make intelligible words. If someone has difficulty with this it may be described as a 'speech difficulty' or 'phonological disorder'.

Another part of form is the grammar of a language. It is important to get the words in the right order if we are going to make sense; for example, 'Tony ate it' and 'it ate Tony' mean different things in English. Grammar also includes word endings (or beginnings, as in 'moral'/'amoral'), which among other things indicate the tense of words, for example 'walk', 'walk<u>ed</u>', and plurals, for example 'cat', 'cat<u>s</u>'. The sequence of words in a sentence is important, as is the sequence of sentences and ideas in a narrative. It is important to say here that grammar, in this sense, is not prescriptive; we're not talking about 'proper' English, just the rules necessary to make words and sentences make sense to a native speaker, regardless of dialect. If someone has difficulty with this it might be described as a 'language difficulty'. We can't necessarily explain the rules of a language we use, but if we are able to use it well then we know them intuitively. However, this kind of metalanguage (using language to talk about language) is increasingly expected in school.

Content

The content of a communication is its meaning. A full knowledge of the structure of a language is of little use unless you are also able to convey meaning and understand others' meaning. (For example, when you learn a foreign language you may be able to construct a grammatical sentence, but you won't be able to use it to talk to someone if you don't know the right vocabulary.) To convey meaning you need a knowledge of vocabulary. However, understanding the content of what people say isn't as simple as learning the meanings of individual words and concepts. We also share meaning through phrases, which can be idiomatic and abstract, such as 'keep your hair on', and by implying meaning. Some examples of the skills necessary to understand and use the content of language are shown in Table 1.2.

Table 1.1 The relevance of 'form' in communication		
	Understanding	*Expressive*
Sound system	Being able to hear the difference between speech sounds and words which sound similar, e.g. 'conclusion' and 'solution'.	Having clear, fluent speech.
Grammar	Being able to recognise and understand the difference between sentences, e.g. 'You can have a sweet' and 'You can have sweets', and 'She hit him' and 'She was hit by him'.	Using grammar appropriately, e.g. 'Yesterday I saw him', rather than 'Yesterday I sawed him'.
Narrative	To understand the sequence of events in a story or a set of instructions.	Organising and expressing ideas in a logical or chronological order.

Table 1.2 The relevance of 'content' in communication		
	Understanding	*Expressive*
Conveying meaning	Being able to understand words, concepts and implied meanings. For example, when the PE teacher says 'Hit it with a bat', it's unlikely that they mean use a small flying rodent. Recognising that idioms such as 'don't hit the ceiling' shouldn't be taken literally.	Being able to find the words you need and use them appropriately in context.

Use

A knowledge of the structure and content of a language is important, but it is not enough; to be a successful communicator you also need a knowledge of the way language is used in a social context. These skills begin to develop before the acquisition of spoken language and are the basis of interactions. In order to use language effectively, verbal and non-verbal communication skills are needed. To be a successful communicator you need to be able to use eye contact and facial expression. You also need to be able to recognise the nuances of meaning that non-verbal communication gives when others are speaking. What's more, to use language appropriately you need an awareness of the person you're talking to, what they might be interested in, their responses to what you say, and the situation. We would talk to a child in a museum very differently to the way we'd talk to our best friend in a pub. Language also has many different functions, such as greeting and protesting, and understanding what these are helps us use language effectively.

Some of the component skills necessary to use language to communicate are detailed in Table 1.3.

Table 1.3 The relevance of 'use' in communication

	Understanding	*Expressive*
Being able to use language to communicate appropriately in context.	Listening and asking for clarification.	Being able to give the right amount of relevant information.
	Understanding the speaker's point of view.	Staying on topic.
	Knowing when it's appropriate for you to take a turn.	Taking turns in a conversation.
		'Repairing' if communication breaks down.
	Looking at and understanding non-verbal feedback.	Showing that you understand by giving verbal and non-verbal feedback.
		Knowing what you can say to a peer and to a teacher.
		Negotiating a part in a game or activity.

Therefore, in order to communicate you need:

- speech which is easily understood
- sentences which are constructed appropriately
- sentences joined logically to make a narrative or story
- memory skills to help you plan what you want to say
- to know and retrieve the appropriate vocabulary
- to understand what others say
- interaction skills and an understanding of the rules of conversation.

And you have to be able to do all of these at once!

The interactive element must not be overlooked either: communication involves joint attention and joint interest plus a desire to share understanding; skills such as watching, listening and waiting, initiation and reciprocation are also crucial (Griffiths 2002). Suffice to say, communicating effectively involves lots of skills which must be used simultaneously.

Language development

Given the number of skills that have to be acquired, learning to communicate is an impressive achievement. Despite this, most children learn language very rapidly. From birth babies are interested in language and communication, though of course they don't yet know which language or languages they will be learning. A baby can hear the prosody of their mother's speech in the womb and this is then recognised once the baby is born. Soon after birth babies show a preference for attending to people rather than anything else and this includes what they say. Gradually through their first year, infants begin to focus on speech that is directed at them, and they also experiment with making sounds and intonations. Between 6 and 12 months babies lose their ability to discriminate speech sounds which are not part of the language they are exposed to. So at this point they focus on their 'mother tongue', which is the particular language people around them are speaking. At ten months babies will babble using sounds from their mother tongue. Babies begin to understand words at between eight to ten months, notwithstanding the fact that they have to work out the appropriate meaning from a large range of possible alternatives. First words are spoken at around a year, and by two years toddlers are linking words (Bates, Thal and Janowsky 1992). At two years old a toddler may be learning nine new words every day, and between 24 and 30 months most of the grammatical features are learnt; this is known as the grammatical explosion (Fenson *et al.* 1994).

Words for feelings and other mental states, such as what you want, think or feel, are abstract and not an obvious grouping of words (such as names for colours), and yet they are also learnt between the ages of two and three. Unsurprisingly, children first use these mental state words to refer to themselves, but by the time they are three they can usually use them to describe others.

As well as developing language rapidly, most children are able to be very creative with it. Children make up words if they don't know them, for example 'blow ball' for balloon. Similarly, deaf children will make up signs if they don't know the ones they need.

Most children starting school can understand 10 to 20 thousand words, their speech is virtually always intelligible, and they can sequence well-formed sentences into simple narratives. They are able to use language to name, classify and reason. They can also use language in sophisticated ways, to establish dominance, to taunt, tease, soothe, and to give or hide information. As they start school, they continue to learn about subtleties of meaning such as double meanings (you can write with a pen and a pig can live in one), and implied requests ('I think it's time to clear up' really means 'Put those toys away now!'). Primary school children may also be learning up to eight new words a day.

Language is both public and private. Vygotsky (1962) described how language is gradually used internally and how, therefore, thinking and inner speech develop as children grow. Language skills continue to increase into adolescence; complex vocabulary and sentence structures are acquired, and such language skills enable literacy to develop. By adolescence, language allows one a means of thinking about feelings and 'rules' of interaction, and provides an acceptance of ambiguity, which results in a realistic representation of the world. Language learning is a continuous lifelong process; it is never finished.

How does language develop?

Language acquisition depends on children being exposed to language and they learn the language of those around them. Children who are deprived of language in their environment do not begin to speak; that much is clear. What hasn't been so easy to determine is the extent to which the ability to learn language is innate, and the extent to which the environment can influence language acquisition. It seems likely that both genetic and environmental influences play a part. It may be that learning form, content and use are not the same things; we don't really know how the grammatical explosion occurs, but learning to use language happens in a social context.

Although exposure to others using a language is important for language acquisition, imitation is only part of the story. Children say things that they are unlikely to have heard from caregivers, such as 'I gived it'. Neither is imitation or simple learning from others a good explanation of how children are able to be creative with language. Some would argue that such creativity is due to an innate understanding of how language works. The fact that all children go through the stages of babbling, and the development of single words and simple sentences, at the same age, regardless of the language they will eventually speak, and evidence that language skills are acquired rapidly and in the same order (Gleason 1997), is taken to support the view that there are innate language abilities in humans. Some have theorised that there are genetically determined 'universal grammars' within our brains, which enable language acquisition. However, no such grammatical universals have been identified. It's more likely that the human brain puts restraints on the characteristics of human languages, and somehow in development these restraints are recognised, and therefore we are able to understand how language works and deduce its rules.

'Motherese'

There seems to be something special about the way people talk to babies and children (and sometimes animals), regardless of whether they are actually the infants' mother. Language directed at children tends to consist of short, simple sentences, presented at a slow pace. It includes lots of repetitions, and is at a higher pitch than usual. There are also more questions and imperatives than would usually be the case (Sachs, Brown and Salerno 1976; Wells and Robinson 1982). These variations on adult speech change in response to the child's perceived developmental level and in response to the child's reactions. This modified language has been described as 'motherese' and 'child directed speech' (Snow 1986).

It is not clear how the child makes use of this modified input; it has been difficult to identify direct effects between the language carers use and children's language development. Parents tend not to respond to the immature grammar of children, but rather to the meaning they are trying to convey. As a consequence, it isn't clear how motherese could affect grammatical development. The importance of motherese has also been called into question because some cultures don't use it. However, babies do seem to prefer to listen to motherese, and they show interest by opening their eyes more in response to these kinds of happy speech patterns. It does seem likely that the child takes an active part in language learning by selectively responding to adult language (Garton 1992). In other words, motherese seems to help a child recognise that this speech is meant for them. It might also help them recognise when it's their turn to speak, as there is often a rising intonation at the end of an adult's turn.

Responsive interactions

Even though there may be some innate abilities that help us learn about the form and function of language, the ability to use language communicatively has to rely on a social context. Feelings and social interactions occur before spoken language and play a part in its development. Caregivers' language to children may not be as important as whether or not they are *responsive* to the child's attempts to communicate. Bruner (1983) considered that interaction is crucial to the language learning process. He felt that a child learns to *use* language rather than learning language in isolation. Language is acquired in a social context. An adult (or another child) will interpret a baby's non-verbal communication and the adult's response will affect the next message. Babies or children may not be intending to influence anyone else, but they learn that they can do so when their vocalisations are interpreted as if they were intentional. It has become widely accepted that responsiveness to a child's communicative attempts is fundamental to language development, rather than exposure to language alone. Interaction has a role in encouraging, facilitating or causing cognitive growth, which includes language development.

The baby or child is an active participant in responsive interactions. Newborn babies are inclined to watch faces and their eyes can just focus on a face when they are held in someone's arms. When infants hear a voice they increase their scanning of a face, particularly the eyes. At three months of age infants can choose where they look, and mutual gaze at this age forms the basis of interactions which will later become verbal. After about six months of age, babies have a vocal repertoire which is both communicative and which expresses emotions that can be recognised by caregivers and used to regulate co-operative interactions (Papaeliou, Minadakis and Cavouras 2002). Most babies have an ability to initiate communicative interchanges by nine months of age, and seem to want to interact and communicate.

The child's temperament is also relevant here as it will affect his or her attention skills, what he or she responds to, and to what degree. Language development seems to be more advanced when a child has good attention control and more positive emotions (Dixon and Smith 2000). Children also have their own language learning styles and those whose early language is more socially oriented learn emotion words more readily than those whose early language is more object related. Predictably, extraversion also seems to be linked to the development of good language skills.

The emotional availability of the mother (or presumably other caregiver) is also a significant factor in the child's language development; it is *responsive* interactions which are important (Kaiser *et al.* 1996). The most important factor as regards language development appears to be the caregiver's willingness to try to expand and understand the child's utterances. (This is also a very important strategy if a child or young person has communication difficulties.)

Responsiveness and interactive turn taking between child and carer provides the 'scaffolding' for the development of vocabulary and grammar. For example, Tamis-Lemonda and Bornstein (1989) found that a caregiver's ability to engage an infant's attention could predict how well that child, as a toddler, could use and understand language. Similarly, three-year-olds who have long conversations and reading sessions with adults have larger vocabularies and better understanding of language than those who do not (Beals, De Temple and Dickinson 1994). However, those with better vocabularies and understanding of language would be able to have longer conversations; it is difficult to disentangle causal relationships.

Interestingly, the responsiveness of early interactions makes it difficult to research the impact of parental input. For example, although mothers typically use lots of internal state words (words which describe feelings and thoughts) to children of two and three years of age, there have been contradictory findings about whether this affects the child's acquisition of such words. Even if a child seemed to learn to use the words his or her mother used frequently, we can't tell whether this was because of the mother using them as a model, or whether the mother used them because she thought the child already understood them, and she was therefore being responsive to the child's feelings.

Emotional development

Bretherton *et al.* (1986) suggest that emotions have developed because of their survival value. They help us understand the meaning of interactions and guide our future behaviour; and they help us understand others and how they might behave in future. To some extent, emotional development seems to be innate, but, as with language development, environmental factors are also relevant. Emotional development is also complex and rapid, emotional skills emerging early and largely developed before a child goes to school.

We all develop primary emotions: disgust, happiness, anger, sadness, surprise and fear. Babies less than a week old can distinguish happy, sad and surprised expressions and they seem to try and imitate them. By 11 weeks, babies are affected by their mother's facial expressions; they freeze in response to fear and show interest in response to a happy face. At three months of age, a baby will react positively to positive speech and negatively to negative talk, so even though they don't understand what we say they understand how it's said. By the age of two, children can talk about emotion in themselves and others, and they can change emotional states through comforting or teasing. At this stage, toddlers also begin to understand that behaviour relates to feelings, that crying might mean someone is sad and that hugs can make people feel better. By five, children can work out how external events have affected others' emotions, that someone might be sad if their hamster has died. However, they may still be perplexed when verbal and non-verbal cues are at odds with each other, so someone saying they feel fine when they look ill will confuse them.

As well as innate ability, emotional attachment and the development of thinking skills are important factors in the development of emotions. Children learn by observing others, considering their own feelings and by talking about them.

Attachment

Human infants are predisposed at birth to seek and make strong emotional bonds with another person, initially in order to stay safe. This drive to connect is probably what lies behind much language and emotional development; we communicate in order to maintain a social contact and to share our feelings and thoughts.

Anxiety triggers the need for affection, comfort and safety and an infant seeks close contact with a caregiver. The caregiver's response to this kind of attachment behaviour is crucial to the child's emotional development. If the response to distress is soothing, it will enable the infant to calm down and then spend time and energy on play, exploration and learning. Other, non-soothing responses may not reduce the child's anxiety. Ainsworth *et al.* (1978) described secure attachment in terms of a relationship where caregivers respond to a child in ways which are predictable and comforting. In secure attachment, a caregiver demonstrates a sensitive response to his or her children's communications and emotional responses, and therefore provides a safe haven. The child feels safe and enjoys interaction with the caregiver; pleasant feelings then become connected with interacting with people in general. In a secure attachment, negative emotions are also met with a sympathetic response, which then allows the child to begin to tolerate these feelings, and to make sense of them and the situation that caused them. Attachment is therefore important for emotional development as it allows the child to work out which emotions can be displayed and how. Attachment also impacts on cognitive growth and provides the foundation for virtually all of the child's psychological development.

Children learn to cope with, express and regulate their own emotions through adults' responses to their expression of emotion. In this way, they also learn to recognise themselves as intentional (that what they do can affect things) and begin to understand their own and others' behaviour. Resilience and self-esteem can also develop as such self-efficacy grows; self-concept develops from the reactions and opinions of others. As a result, preschool children who are securely attached are more sociable and empathic towards others; they are also less hostile and anxious and have more social support and resilience than those who are not. Factors within the child are relevant here, as we all have different temperaments from birth. Unsurprisingly, children with difficult temperaments elicit more negative interactions and those with easy temperaments receive more positive responses.

There is evidence that children who are securely attached understand emotions better than those who are not (De Rosnay and Harris 2002). The same is true of communication skills; mothers' attuned responses (that is, where their responses show that they have understood what the child feels) to their children's feelings promote earlier language development. There also seems to be a correlation between security of attachment and general language measures (Cicchetti and Beeghly 1987). For example, Gesten *et al.* (1986) found that securely attached toddlers used more complex language than did cognitively matched, maltreated children. Secure attachment may facilitate language development, but language is also important for attachment development. Language can be used to express feelings and intentions as well as enabling children to understand about their caregivers' future availability – for example, when a mother says, 'I will pick you up from nursery.' Language is also one way that anxieties can be soothed, initially by the caregiver, then eventually by the child him- or herself. Securely attached children learn that they can communicate about their feelings and their mental state and that this will lead to predictable and desired outcomes (Crittenden 1995), because they are listened to and responded to. Securely attached children can thereby gain meaning from the integration of feelings and thoughts.

Through a secure attachment, children can gain basic care, safety, emotional warmth, stimulation, guidance and boundaries, and stability (Department of Health/Department for Education and Employment/Home Office 2000). This kind of attachment confers considerable resilience to adversity and enables children to grow up to be effective and positive parents themselves. Secure caregiving is not just about responsiveness but also mind mindedness (responding to babies or children as if they have a mind), and developing a theory of mind also seems to be an important part of emotional development.

Theory of mind

A theory of mind is essential for working out why people behave the way they do. We assume that others think and feel as we do (though they may not have the same thoughts and feelings in response to the same event as we do) and that this affects their behaviour. Therefore we infer mental states from behaviour and this affects the way we communicate with other people. We recognise when someone is not listening to us, or when they're excited, pretending or being silly, and we react accordingly.

As children develop, they begin to recognise that they have desires and goals and that these affect the way they behave. They also learn that others have similar desires and goals and that they also act in response to them; they realise that others have minds too. Caregivers' behaviour is important in helping a child to develop a theory of mind. This happens when they treat the child as intentional through meaningful interpretations of early vocalisations; in other words, the baby makes a gurgle and the caregiver responds with, for example, 'Are you hungry?' Caregivers also help to develop a theory of mind in children through a propensity to focus on the thoughts and feelings of the child. If caregivers are mind minded – that is, they respond to children and babies by assuming they have feelings and intentions – then they will be able to help children recognise their own feelings, regulate them and understand them in others (Fonagy and Target 1997). There is a link between children developing a theory of mind, and the development of language to describe thoughts, feelings and beliefs or mental state words. As children acquire a theory of mind, their understanding of mental state words develops and they are more likely to refer to mental states of their friends and siblings (Patnaik and Babu 2001).

The presence of a theory of mind can be shown in the 'false belief task'. In the false belief task, the child sees another person witness a toy being hidden. Once this person has left the room, someone else moves the toy. The child's task is to say where the original witness thinks the toy is, not where it is now. Children are only able to do this if they appreciate that the person who left the room did not see the toy being moved; they have to realise that another person's experiences were different from their own. Children and young people with autism will assume that the person who left the room knows that the toy was moved, though they can't have seen it happening. Autistic children have difficulty developing a theory of mind and therefore assume that others' experience is the same as their own.

Emotional intelligence

Emotional intelligence is a similar concept to mind mindedness and is a useful way of describing the skills necessary to function well emotionally. It seems likely that emotional intelligence skills are important in an individual's success in many areas of life. Our culture has tended to prize logical/mathematical and linguistic intelligence. However, individuals who have high intelligence in these 'traditional' areas, but who are lacking in emotional intelligence, are not necessarily successful either in terms of relationships or work, because most of what we do involves interactions with others and this requires an understanding of emotions. Although there has been a body of thought that has tried to separate logical thought from emotions, it seems that this is unrealistic, and even if it were possible it would not be beneficial, as emotions influence thought. Our emotions affect everything we do and influence the way we think. For example, exams are about assessing what we have learnt, but students who can manage their anxiety and motivate themselves to prepare well are more likely to be successful than those who know the subject well, but who are overwhelmed by their fears about exams. Emotions can speed up or enhance the thinking process when one is feeling confident, but in times of great stress the brain can go into survival mode, and thinking can be impaired.

The idea of 'emotional intelligence' has grown from the recognition that there is more than one type of intelligence. Gardner (1983) describes the following kinds of intelligence:

- linguistic
- logical mathematical
- bodily kinaesthetic
- musical
- spatial
- interpersonal
- intrapersonal.

Emotional intelligence is interpersonal and intrapersonal and it enables us to understand our own and others' emotions. Emotional intelligence is about recognising that we are emotional and learning to understand and manage our emotions.

The concept of emotional intelligence has begun to influence thinking in the areas of education, health and management. As regards education, the best learning environments enable students to feel safe, confident and exploratory, much as a caregiver in a secure attachment does. Good teachers remember that learning can be frightening, that it takes courage to try something new and potentially difficult, and that one might be beset with doubts about one's ability. Children (and probably the rest of us) learn more in positive affective states; that is, when we are happy and confident. Concentration, planning and problem-solving can all be affected by emotions, so their regulation is crucial for learning.

There are clear links between our emotions and our physical well-being. Constant emotional upset is a health risk. There seem to be links between emotional stress and both heart disease and a suppressed immune system. Research in this area has found that being able to calm yourself when ill and anxious is a vital emotional tool and also that optimism has healing power. This seems to resonate with ideas about secure attachment; perhaps the soothing received as an infant enables one to learn to soothe oneself and be hopeful in later life. Having supporting relationships also helps people cope with illness, and emotional intelligence is likely to be important in forming such relationships.

Another area where emotional skills are important is at work. Emotionally intelligent management, that which considers the feelings of the workforce and how these might affect their ability to work, is more effective and often more profitable. Teamwork in particular is most effective if the members of the team are emotionally intelligent, because social harmony makes the team successful. Motivation can also be seen as an emotional intelligence skill as it is about managing one's emotions in order to achieve a goal.

Links between language and emotional development

Brain development

Language and emotional development, and indeed the development of thinking, depend on the growth of the brain, which quadruples in size during childhood. Any factors which influence the development of the brain could also influence emotional and language development.

This rapid growth in the brain, combined with observations about the rate of language learning in childhood, has led to ideas about 'critical periods'. It seemed that the critical period for learning language was before adolescence. In other words, if language hadn't developed in childhood, then it was unlikely to. It is certainly true that young children learn new languages (including sign languages) faster than older children or adults (so why do we begin learning additional languages in secondary school?). Also, evidence from studies of brain damage affecting speech show that before ten years of age children are likely to recover their language, but after age 12 only 60 per cent recovered language. However, language learning does continue into adolescence and probably into adulthood (Nippold 1993). The more we learn about the brain, the more it seems that the brain's potential to develop is unlimited, so although early brain growth is important for language and emotional development, such development can occur in later years.

External influences can affect the way the brain develops. Connections in the developing brain are pruned or strengthened depending on how much they are used, so the environment, including early interactions, can therefore affect brain structure and function. Cognitive, or thinking, skills can also influence the development of communication and emotional skills. For example, much early interaction is dependent on the development of the infant's ability to share attention; that is, to be able to focus on what someone else is looking at, so that the infant and caregiver both give attention to the same thing. This is a deceptively simple skill, but if it is not in place, interactions will be impaired. Temperament and personality are also relevant; some of us are more inclined to communicate than others, and the way we respond to others will affect their interactions with us.

Other cognitive skills, such as memory and processing, are necessary for language development, particularly those which affect the ability to process speech. In order to learn language, it is necessary to be able to attend to language that is heard, to process it and gain meaning from it. Children who have specific language impairment seem to have limitations that disrupt language processing, particularly when stimuli are presented rapidly (Gillam and Hoffman 2000). Therefore, it seems that intact information processing skills are important for language development.

Language and emotional development could not occur without the massive brain development which occurs early in infancy, but clearly it is not just an increase in the capacity of the brain that allows for development – specific cognitive skills are important, and input from the environment also influences the way the brain grows and develops.

Play and interaction

Play and interaction are important in the development of both emotional and communication skills; indeed, the development of these skills is intertwined. Play is a way of expressing emotions, letting off steam, learning adult roles and is important for language development. Through play, children learn about the use of symbols; toys represent real things. Language is a more complex form of symbolic representation, which develops as symbolic play becomes more sophisticated. Pretend play, with accompanying talk, may help discussions of difficult emotions such as fear and anger which could be difficult in other contexts (Haight and Sachs 1995).

Interaction and play with peers is also crucial for the development of emotional and language skills, and vice versa. Children who use more emotion words are more likely to be popular (Fabes et al. 2001). This is no doubt linked to the idea that good socialisers are those who are able to regulate their emotions well. Social interaction is therefore important for the development of many skills relevant to language and emotional development, such as turn taking and considering others' points of view, but it also requires skills in these areas.

Links between language and emotional development

There haven't been many theories that have attempted to explain how language and emotional development could interact. Although language has long been accepted as relevant to thinking and social interaction, the importance of language for emotional functioning has only been acknowledged more recently.

Perhaps the most obvious link between emotion and language is that language is important for expressing and regulating internal states. Although we can think non-verbally, we tend to think about how we feel and share our feelings in words (Dale 1996). Some evidence for this comes from Bloom and Beckwith (1989), who considered the integration of language and emotion. Their observations suggest that the rate of a child's language development is strongly influenced by the child's emotional state. They studied two-year-olds and found that they could express positive or negative emotions directly, by laughing or crying, or, when they were in a neutral emotional state, they were able to use words. The two-year-olds in this study could not communicate verbally in conditions of emotional arousal, nor could they communicate in words about emotions (when upset or excited). Therefore, Bloom and Beckwith argue that the rate of early language development is correlated to the amount of time a child spends in neutral affect expression (in a calm state); situations of great anxiety or excitement, therefore, might impair language development, particularly if they are prolonged.

Greenberg *et al.* (1995) have suggested a model of integration between emotional and language development. Initially, a baby's needs and emotions are directly expressed through behaviour and it is not until about the age of three that, as language develops, there is some symbolic mediation between the feeling and the behaviour. In other words, language can provide a moment of contemplation between the experience of an emotion and its expression. At this stage, the child can recognise and label basic emotions, and this is the beginning of reflective social planning and problem-solving. From around the age of six, thinking in words has become habitual, as has an increasing ability to reflect on and plan sequences of actions. Children of this age are also beginning to consider multiple consequences of actions, and part of any consequence is consideration of the emotions the situation might evoke. In adolescence, these skills develop further, so that multiple perspectives can be considered simultaneously; again, this requires an understanding of the emotions and thoughts of various people and the language to describe this. Therefore, it seems that language is a vital part of emotional development and emotional intelligence, as it can provide a moment of delay which can lead to a situation being dealt with in a way other than an immediate response through action.

Greenberg *et al.* (1995) assume that the emergence of these new emotional and language skills is largely dependent on adult–child interaction. It seems that children with strong attachments do develop better cognitive and language skills (Robinson and Acevedo 2001).

It is also important to remember that children and young people talk to each other and learn from each other. Their conversations are different from those with adults; they talk about mental states more with other children than with their parents and even more with friends (Brown and Donelan-McCall 1993). Kopp (1989) also observed that children talked about feelings in pretend play with others, and through this they began to understand more about how to deal with feelings, especially difficult ones.

Conclusion

Traditionally, language and emotional development have been studied separately and often by different professionals using incompatible theoretical frameworks. However, language and emotional development occur together within an individual and they affect each other powerfully. Another important factor to consider is that both language and emotional development can be influenced by the environment, and in particular the relationships between carers and a developing child. Complex skills such as co-operation, self-control and language are learnt through interactions with a caregiver, usually before the age of five (Kaiser *et al.* 2000). If these are not in place, much subsequent development is jeopardised. Individual differences within children will also affect the way their language and emotional skills develop.

CHAPTER 2

The Links Between Communication Difficulties and Emotional and Behavioural Problems

Are there links between communication difficulties and emotional and behavioural problems?

The development of communication and emotional skills is a complicated intertwining process, so it isn't surprising that problems can occur and that difficulties in either domain can influence the development of the other. What is surprising is the lack of research to explore these influences. What has become more and more apparent is that communication and emotional and behavioural problems often occur together. Before considering the reasons for this co-occurrence, I would like to clarify what I mean by communication and emotional and behavioural difficulties.

Defining emotional and behavioural problems

The term 'emotional and behavioural difficulties' encompasses many different kinds of problems, so it is important to be clear at the outset that this is not a homogeneous group of children and young people. Generalisations about the 'EBD' population are therefore flawed. There are various definitions and classifications of emotional and behavioural difficulties used by different disciplines. 'Emotional and behavioural disorders' and 'mental health difficulties' are overlapping and interchangeable terms, probably used to refer to some of the same children and young people. Certainly the definitions for these terms used by health and educational workers are similar, though they don't use the same terminology.

The American Psychiatric Association's (1994) Diagnostic and Statistical Manual of Mental Disorders (DSM-IV) classification tends to predominate in the literature on child psychiatry. However, the International Classification of

Diseases (ICD-10) (World Health Organisation 1994) is also used, particularly in Europe, and has similar categories of disorder to DSM. The DSM categories include developmental, behavioural and emotional disorders. Some of these are as follows and some have self-explanatory titles:

1. Developmental Disorders

    (a) Pervasive Developmental Disorder (PDD) is characterised by impairment of interactions, communication skills and imaginative activity. Autism is seen as a severe form of PDD. Asperger's syndrome/disorder is also included in this category; the communication difficulties, which are part of this, are subtler in nature than those in autism.

2. Behavioural Disorders

    (a) Attention Deficit Hyperactivity Disorder (ADHD) consists of impulsivity, developmentally inappropriate inattention and hyperactivity. Attention deficit disorder can also occur where there is no hyperactivity.

    (b) Oppositional Defiant Disorder.

    (c) Conduct Disorder.

3. Emotional Disorders

    (a) Overanxious Disorder.

    (b) Dysthymia is a chronic disturbance of mood, including depression.

Other disorders included in the DSM classification system which may be relevant to the relationship between EBD and communication difficulties are:

- Reactive Attachment Disorder
- Selective Mutism
- Schizophrenia
- Post-traumatic Stress Disorder.

Emotional and behavioural problems can also be categorised into externalising problems, which include aggressive and antisocial behaviour, and internalising problems, which include anxiety and depression. Boys are more likely to have externalising disorders such as ADHD and Conduct Disorder, whereas girls are more likely to have internalising difficulties such as depression or anxiety. Other relevant aspects of the child such as medical conditions, psychosocial adversity and specific delays in development can be included in the DSM or ICD classification, in what is known as a multi-axial scheme. This is useful because one 'diagnosis' is often inadequate in describing the difficulties a child faces; they may have specific difficulty with reading, moderate learning difficulties, Conduct Disorder, epilepsy, communication difficulties and depression.

In the UK, children and young people who have emotional and behavioural difficulties are not always referred for a psychiatric assessment, nor are they necessarily given clear diagnoses like those in DSM-IV or ICD-10. A psychiatric referral is more likely if they seem to have a specific 'syndrome' or very puzzling behaviour; otherwise, a medical diagnosis may not be seen as beneficial. One of the problems with these diagnoses is immediately apparent; they imply that children who have emotional or behavioural problems have psychiatric difficulty or mental illness, when this is not always the case. Furthermore, some of the diagnoses don't seem to be that useful. Having the diagnosis 'Conduct Disorder' (comprising a wide variety of defiant, aggressive and antisocial behaviours) does not benefit the child or family (except if it leads to appropriate treatment, which if it does, is unlikely to be medical in nature). Also, even if young people have the same 'symptoms' of Conduct Disorder, these may have occurred for widely differing reasons (Moffit *et al.* 1996) and this wider context should not be overlooked. Some argue that labelling all behavioural problems as mental health difficulties diverts doctors into work which is really the responsibility of others (Goodman 1997). However, multi-axial classifications like DSM are useful for guiding treatment, gathering information and for research. If enough information is collected and recorded about young people's presenting emotional and behavioural problems, as well as other relevant aspects such as psychosocial adversity, we may begin to see patterns and this could help in the understanding of the links between emotional, behavioural and communication difficulties.

For many children, the 'diagnosis' of emotional and behavioural difficulties is an educational one, arrived at through the special educational needs procedure, often without reference to child mental health services; in effect, it is that they cannot be educated in an ordinary classroom without additional support. However, getting a 'statement of special educational needs' can be very difficult and there is no standard procedure across local educational authorities. A formal definition of 'emotionally and behaviourally disordered' children comes from the Department of Education (England). It says that their behaviours are problematic regardless of the situation or the people involved. The following key areas are identified:

- disruptive anti-social and aggressive behaviour
- hyperactivity
- concentration and attention difficulties
- somatic difficulties
- emotional and related problems.

These difficulties can take the form of:

- withdrawal
- depressive or suicidal tendencies
- eating disorders
- school phobia
- substance misuse
- frustration and anger
- threat of, or actual, violence.

(Department for Education and Skills 2001b, paragraphs 3.65–3.66)

There is also an awareness that interactions between social and psychological factors, as well as factors within the child, can contribute to emotional and behavioural difficulties, leading to the use of the term 'social, emotional and behavioural difficulties' in the draft revised Special Educational Needs code of practice (Department for Education and Skills 2001a). In effect, the term 'emotional and behavioural difficulties' encompasses children and young people who may not have very much in common: those whose behaviour is unacceptable, those who are under stress as well as those who are mentally ill.

Children who have externalising difficulties (mostly boys) are more likely to be referred for extra help, while those with primarily emotional or internalising difficulties (mostly girls) are ignored. However, the 'emotional' part of the definition is very important; to consider the behaviour alone ignores the reasons why it may occur. Unacceptable behaviour leads to negative responses from others which can further lower self-esteem and add to emotional difficulties. Basically, these are children who are both troubled and troubling. Having the label 'emotional and behavioural difficulties' is often seen as a disgrace and a sign of deficit by the young people themselves (Cooper 1996).

Defining communication difficulties

There are various ways of defining and categorising communication difficulties, but none so clear-cut as the DSM. Although there are broad categories of communication problems included in the DSM categorisation, such as mixed receptive-expressive language disorder and stuttering, these fail to capture the heterogeneous nature of communication difficulties. The use of such categories, which underestimate the complexity of communication problems, may have made it more difficult to find links between communication difficulties and emotional and behavioural problems.

One way of considering communication difficulties is by dividing them into speech disorders as opposed to language disorders. Speech disorders encompass conditions which lead to unintelligibility, including voice disorders. 'Voice disorders' are those in which the quality of the voice is impaired due to organic or functional reasons, or a combination of both. Language disorders can be divided into problems with understanding language, known as receptive language problems or comprehension difficulties, and problems with expressive language.

Sometimes a communication difficulty can be described as a language 'delay' because the course of typical development is followed but at a later age than is usually the case. A language disorder occurs where the course of typical development is not followed, though in practice language delay and disorder often occur together. Some children have what is termed a 'specific language impairment', where language difficulties occur in the absence of any other impairment; however, such a definition is problematic because language impairment may lead on to other problems through its effect on learning and interaction. It is more likely that a young person with communication difficulties will be male, although that could be because communication problems in girls are under-detected (Tomblin *et al.* 1997). Communication difficulties are not only many and varied but they can change over time. Some children have transient language delay and some have communication difficulties which persist.

There are some clearly definable communication disorders such as verbal or articulatory dyspraxia, which is a disorder of planning where the messages from the brain are 'scrambled', leading to difficulty co-ordinating the muscles for speech. However, having this diagnosis does not exclude the possibility of additional communication problems. There are also postulated subtypes of communication disorders such as syntactic-phonologic (where there is difficulty using sounds in words and grammar and word endings appropriately) or semantic-pragmatic (where there is difficulty with content and use) types, but the existence of these is still debated and children's problems often fit into more than one category. Research is continuing to try and find categorisations of communication difficulties; these would be useful in identifying the best kind of speech and language therapy and what the long-term outcomes might be.

It is possible to have difficulty with the form, content or use of language, or indeed all three. Most young people with communication problems have patterns of difficulty that are quite individual. Some examples of communication problems are as follows. It is important to note that comprehension difficulties can occur in all areas. The more areas involved, the less likely is a positive outcome.

Difficulties with form:

- Speech which is difficult to understand.
- Problems discriminating speech sounds, so 'catch' and 'cat' might sound the same.
- Grammatical immaturity; using sentence structures more appropriate for someone younger.
- Problems linking sentences with words such as 'and', 'but', 'so', 'then' etc.
- Difficulty understanding complex sentences such as passives; for example, 'The boy was kicked by the girl.' Since the first person mentioned in a sentence is usually the one who is active, someone with communication difficulties might think the boy did the kicking.
- Difficulty sequencing sentences to make a meaningful narrative.

Difficulties with content:

- Problems learning new words.
- Difficulty retrieving known words at the right time; also known as 'word finding' difficulties.
- Difficulty understanding idioms such as 'Don't hit the ceiling'.
- Limited vocabulary for emotion words.
- Being unable to identify the key theme or topic.

Difficulties with use:

- Limited eye contact.
- Poor turn-taking and starting and ending conversations.
- Problems 'repairing' when two people talk at once or misunderstand each other.
- Unable to understand or respond to feedback from the listener.
- Unable to stay on topic in conversation.
- Problems with verbal negotiation.

(The charities Afasic and I CAN both produce information leaflets about communication difficulties.)

Communication difficulties and emotional and behavioural problems often occur together

There is mounting evidence for a link between communication difficulties and emotional and behavioural problems. Of those children who have communication difficulties, 50 to 75 per cent are likely to develop emotional and behavioural problems and psychiatric difficulties of all kinds. This means they are three to four times more likely to develop such difficulties than other children. Sixty to ninety-five per cent of children who have emotional and behavioural difficulties are also likely to have communication difficulties (Baker and Cantwell 1987; Camarata, Hughes and Rhul 1988). This raises the question, why are the two so closely linked?

There are many ways in which emotional and behavioural problems and communication difficulties could, theoretically, be linked. Communication problems could cause emotional and behavioural problems, or emotional and behavioural problems could cause communication difficulties. There are also factors which could cause both emotional and communication difficulties; attachment problems could affect language and emotional development, and attention deficit disorder is perhaps a manifestation of a cognitive deficit which affects both behaviour and language development. Environmental factors also impact on language and emotional development; low socio-economic status and child abuse put children at risk of linguistic and emotional impairment. For many children affected by emotional and behavioural problems and communication difficulties, several of these links could occur together.

Do communication problems cause emotional and behavioural difficulties?

There is some persuasive evidence for the idea that communication problems can cause emotional and behavioural difficulties, or at least that behavioural problems develop subsequent to communication difficulties. Researchers have found that children with communication disorders are more likely to develop behavioural difficulties and psychiatric illness than their peers (Clegg, Hollis and Rutter 1999; Silva, Williams and McGee 1987).

Several longitudinal studies have also suggested a link between early communication difficulties and subsequent emotional and behavioural problems. Beitchman *et al.* (1989) found that children who had language difficulties at age five (particularly problems understanding language) were more likely to have behavioural difficulties at age 12 than their peers. Rutter and Mawhood (1991) followed the development of 20 boys who were diagnosed as having developmental language disorders in the 1960s. As adults, a third of these men had developed social and psychiatric difficulties. Also, Davison and Howlin (1997), in a follow-up study of children who had attended a primary language unit, noted that there was an increase in behavioural, social and emotional problems as these children got older.

How could communication problems lead on to emotional and behavioural difficulties?

We have all experienced frustration over communication difficulties, so it is possible to understand how they might lead to behavioural outbursts. Caulfield (1989) tested this 'frustration' hypothesis by giving children who had communication difficulties a task that was particularly taxing for them, a naming task. Unsurprisingly, they were more likely to misbehave when faced with such a task that they could not complete. Similar situations frequently occur in classrooms where children with communication difficulties are unable to meet the language demands of the lesson.

For some children with communication difficulties, emotional problems rather than behavioural difficulties are the long-term result. This seems to happen because of the isolating effect of having communication difficulties. Rutter and Mawhood (1991) found that the main increase in psychopathology over time in language-impaired individuals was due to anxiety, problems with social relationships and attention deficit difficulties, rather than conduct disorders. Evidence for the preponderance of emotional difficulties also comes from a study of children who had specific language impairments at a special school (Haynes and Naidoo 1991). High rates of behaviours which were indicative of frustration declined quite rapidly, but problems associated with low self-confidence, low self-esteem and social withdrawal remained.

The association between communication difficulties and emotional and behavioural difficulties seems to vary depending on the type of communication problem. If the communication difficulty is isolated to the ability to produce intelligible speech, then the association is at its weakest. This may be because many such 'speech' problems are resolved early, even though they can cause considerable frustration in the short term. However, some children who have apparently resolved 'speech' or phonological problems may go on to develop literacy difficulties. The risk of literacy difficulties is higher for children with communication problems, and school failure of this kind has also been shown to lead on to behaviour problems.

There is also a greater association between communication disorders and behaviour problems when the children involved have difficulty constructing language to express themselves (rather than when their speech is unintelligible) and particularly when they have difficulty understanding language (Baker and Cantwell 1987; Whitehurst and Fischel 1994).

Toppelberg (2000) reviewed the previous ten years of research in child language and communication disorders and concluded that receptive language disorders are high-risk indicators for later psychiatric difficulties. Botting and Conti-Ramsden (2000) assessed over two hundred children with language impairment and found that those with complex language problems (i.e. difficulty with both understanding language and expressing themselves) were most likely to have a clinical level of behavioural difficulty.

So it seems to be the case that where there are complex or severe communication difficulties (including the ability to understand language) externalising or behaviour problems become more common, in addition to the internalising difficulties of anxiety. There also seems to be a link between poor auditory comprehension and aggression. Aggression can develop in many ways. Young people who do not understand what others say to them feel frustrated and inept, and they might respond aggressively (Sigafoos 2000). Those who have poor understanding of language seem likely to develop hyperactive symptoms, and boys in this group are also likely to be aggressive. This may be because they have difficulty attending in class, and their behaviour is seen as unacceptable, which causes them further frustration

(Beitchman *et al.* 1996). Children who have problems understanding language may inappropriately believe themselves to be the object of ridicule, and therefore resort to violence (Beitchman 1985). Language is a key factor in the self-regulation of behaviour. So, verbal deficits may mean that children do not develop the inner speech which helps them plan and modify behaviour, thus making them more likely to have behavioural outbursts.

Difficulties with the use of language are particularly relevant here because of its importance for social interactions (Sanger, Maag and Shapera 1994). Unfortunately, communication problems impair interaction and, then as a consequence, children with communication problems may be rejected by their peers and even bullied or scape-goated. This can initiate a negative spiral of interactions where the child with communication difficulties finds it increasingly difficult to interact in a positive way (Rice 1993). Thus, children and young people with communication problems are at risk of negative inter-actions, which can bring about and maintain behavioural difficulties.

Some would argue that the ways children with communication difficulties behave are adaptations to their language limitations rather than behaviour problems per se (Redmond and Rice 1998). Compensatory behaviours, which may be seen as behaviour problems, can actually result from the communica-tive demands of the situation, the child's verbal abilities and the biases and behaviours of people within their environment, rather than from emotional or psychiatric problems. In other words, language-impaired children are likely to be less responsive to language, and initiate less than their peers, as well as relying on adults to help out where they are unable to negotiate verbally. These behaviours can be interpreted as immaturity or evidence of an internal-ising disorder. This kind of misinterpretation is discussed further in the next chapter. It is undoubtedly the case that children with communication difficul-ties are often misunderstood and seen as solely immature or behaving inap-propriately.

One major implication is that in many children with 'behavioural' problems, verbal difficulties are primary and their remediation could ameliorate the behavioural difficulties. Simple measures can make a great deal of difference. Identifying and understanding communication difficulties is a first step (see Chapter 3). If adults speaking to children with communication problems reduce the linguistic complexity of their speech, this can also result in positive behavioural changes (Prizant *et al.* 1990).

Do emotional and behavioural problems cause communication difficulties?

There is not a great deal of evidence for emotional and behavioural problems being a direct cause of communication difficulties. However, there are 'psychiatric' difficulties where communication problems coexist and are part of the diagnosis, for example in selective mutism, autism, Tourette's syndrome and schizophrenia. There also seems to be a close association between attention deficit disorder and communication problems.

Selective mutism

Selective mutism may seem to be an example of a psychiatric problem producing communication difficulties, though causation is often more complex than it first appears. It is very rare, occurring in probably less than 1 per cent of all children and young people. It occurs where a child finds verbal communication difficult in one or more situations, while being able to communicate well in other environments. Often selective mutism begins when a child starts school and the child does not talk in school, or in the presence of unfamiliar people, although they have no difficulty with talking at home amongst their family. Anxiety about the new environment seems to be the precipitating factor here. Children who develop selective mutism often have a history of anxiety in social situations. Selective mutism is seen as a social phobia, a kind of anxiety disorder. Once a child has been unable to speak at school for a while, the pattern is often difficult to break. The title of this disorder has been changed from elective mutism to selective mutism to reflect the fact that the child does not consciously choose to be mute.

So, is selective mutism a psychiatric disorder which causes communication difficulties? It may be in some cases. However, children who are selectively mute often have an underlying communication impairment, and many have English as an additional language, so it is not clear whether the emotional difficulty is primary. Some children are already anxious because of communication difficulties and the additional stress of starting school precipitates mutism (Cline and Baldwin 1994). In addition, there is often some kind of emotional risk factor in children who are selectively mute (Champagne and Cronk 1998), such as attachment difficulties or emotional or physical immaturity, which might also lead to communication difficulties. Also, MacGregor, Pullar and Cundall (1994) found that 5 out of 18 children in their study of selective mutes had suffered from abuse (though this is the only study to have found a higher than average rate). So, as yet, it has not been possible to untangle the emotional, behavioural and linguistic factors which lead to selective mutism.

Post-traumatic Stress Disorder

Post-traumatic Stress Disorder can disrupt communication and attention. Someone who has experienced severe trauma may become mute as they re-experience (or remember) that trauma as part of Post-traumatic Stress Disorder. This kind of mutism is a temporary communication problem that results from an extremely emotionally stressful situation. Such 'hysteria' or conversion disorder in children may lead to a loss of voice, mutism or dysfluency, but it is very rare (Jones 1996), and is therefore unlikely to be relevant to the large numbers of children who have both emotional and com-munication difficulties. More significantly, there may be a permanent change in brain chemistry in children due to trauma (Perry *et al.* 1995; Rauch *et al.* 1996) and this could theoretically affect communication in the longer term, particularly if it alters information processing. If trauma is persistent, then the fear state it produces also becomes persistent, resulting in a child who is hypervigilant, focused on threat-related cues (which are mainly non-verbal), anxious and impulsive. These behaviours may be useful in a threatening situation, but not once it has passed. Hypervigilant children find it difficult to learn and to interact and it seems likely that this will have significant negative effects on their development in all areas. Therefore, Post-traumatic Stress Disorder is a psychiatric problem which could potentially impair both com-munication and emotional development. A healthy attachment can protect a child from the worst effects of trauma because the child has a basic sense of trust, has learnt some self-soothing and can look to caretakers for comfort. Conversely, children with poor attachment may be affected more severely. Young people are not more able to recover from trauma than adults, even though they may appear to because they may express their distress differently.

Autism

The causes of autism are still unclear, though they result in a neurological or biological problem, which leads to distinct difficulties in the areas of commu-nication (mainly in terms of its use rather than its form), social interaction and stereotypical behaviour. Some argue that the fundamental deficit in autism is with shared attention and theory of mind (Baron-Cohen 1995). This results in a limited ability to build shared understandings of events, and to talk about them, because the person with autism may have difficulty appreciating others' perspectives, focus of attention or internal motivations such as thoughts and feelings (Sigman and Capps 1997). So autism is an emotional and behavioural difficulty where communication problems are part of the diagnosis. Since the cause is unclear, it is impossible to say whether this is a psychiatric difficulty that causes communication difficulty, or vice versa. Both probably result from early cognitive deficits.

Tourette's syndrome

Tourette's syndrome is characterised by tics, which are involuntary, rapid and repetitive movements. Tourette's is diagnosed when such tics persist for more than a year. These tics usually appear before adulthood. Initially they are non-verbal, but later verbal tics appear as well. Verbal tics include explosive repetitive verbalisations, throat clearing and grunting, and they may be obscene in nature. Tourette's syndrome often co-occurs with Attention Deficit Hyperactivity Disorder (ADHD) and it can also lead to behavioural outbursts.

The communication difficulties of children with Tourette's syndrome is an under-researched area. Verbal tics can certainly impair interaction, although children with this syndrome often have relatively intact communication skills. Again, this syndrome is too rare to account for much of the association between communication and emotional and behavioural difficulties.

Schizophrenia

Schizophrenia involves delusions, hallucinations or disturbances in emotion and thought. People with schizophrenia have been described as having a dysfunction in thought and in linguistic organisation (among other symptoms), in particular with the speaker–hearer role relationship, as they do not always orientate the listener appropriately and this can make their speech difficult to follow (Andreason 1979). Onset is usually in adolescence or early adulthood. However, Caplan (1996) has studied the discourse (or narrative skills) of schizophrenic children and they seem to have problems with organisation, both at the level of topic maintenance and reasoning and also at the linguistic level of linking sentences. Children with schizophrenia are also likely to have difficulty understanding abstract language as well as having auditory processing deficits. They may also have voice (nasality or breathiness),

∿   ,otonous intonation) and fluency problems (Baltaxe and
                 95).

        ,unication difficulties are a core feature of schizophrenia but they
          ,ear before the psychiatric difficulty, so the latter is unlikely to be the
    ι   . Individuals who go on to develop schizophrenia often have delayed
language development, as well as other developmental problems. Cannon *et
al.* (2002) found that impairments in neuromotor skills, receptive language,
and cognitive development are present among children later diagnosed as
having schizophreniform disorder.

In schizophrenia, thought is affected, but thought processes are expressed
through language, so is it possible to tell whether the language or thought
disorder is fundamental? Is it possible to tell the difference between
disordered language and disordered thought? Poor cohesion within and
across sentences is also seen in language-impaired children and is seen as a
linguistic/structural deficit. The likelihood is that thought and language are
inextricably intertwined and this underlines the importance of a good differential diagnosis, not only for potentially schizophrenic children but for all
children with emotional and behavioural as well as communication difficulties.

Attention Deficit Hyperactivity Disorder

Attention Deficit Hyperactivity Disorder (ADHD) is the most common psychiatric disorder in childhood (Anderson *et al.* 1987). Some would argue that
this might be because it is overdiagnosed and the overlap with communication difficulties could be relevant to this. ADHD is characterised by developmentally inappropriate levels of attention, impulsiveness and hyperactivity
which cannot be accounted for by cognitive (intellectual) level, developmental level or by other disorders (e.g. psychosis or affective disorder). In
ADHD, poor attention, impulsiveness and hyperactivity cause significant
impairment of social, or academic, functioning. It is not easy to diagnose
ADHD; all of us are inattentive, impulsive and overactive at times. The levels
of these behaviours have to be unusual and handicapping. ADHD is also easy
to confuse with other difficulties. Inattention can also be characteristic of
Post-traumatic Stress Disorder, Reactive Attachment Disorder, Oppositional
Defiant Disorder, Conduct Disorder, learning difficulties and neurological
dysfunction.

Although there seems to be a close association between communication
and psychiatric problems, there are no clear links between any particular com-

munication problem and emotional and behavioural difficulty. However, the psychiatric problem most commonly associated with communication difficulties is ADHD (Cantwell and Baker 1991). Children who have ADHD have often had delayed language development, and they may have residual expressive language difficulties and problems understanding language. Even though some of them may talk a great deal, in situations where there are specific demands on them, for example when they are asked to describe or explain something, they become less fluent and their language becomes disorganised. Children and young people who have ADHD often find it difficult to organise their ideas into a coherent narrative and they are also unlikely to use internal speech.

Tannock, Purvis and Schachar (1993) found that pragmatic (use of language) difficulties are evident in the majority of children with ADHD, even in those whose other language skills are well developed. For example, these children do not always respond to questions or requests, and are likely to interrupt others. They give less feedback in conversation and have difficulty monitoring the listener's understanding of what they have said (Kim 1999). They also seem to find it difficult to alter their communication style in response to the speaker or the situation. Buitelaar *et al.* (1994) characterised hyperactive children as having a primary deficit in social attention. So the link between ADHD and communication problems may be strongest as regards the 'use' of language.

There are various estimates of the degree of overlap between attention deficits and communication problems, depending on the type of study and the definition of ADHD used. Love and Thompson (1988) found that about 75 per cent of children with language delay also had attention deficits. Serious behaviour problems were also found in just over half of children with language delays in a study by Baker and Cantwell (1987); behavioural immaturity and over-activity were particularly common. Beitchman *et al.* (1989) observed an association of 30 per cent between communication problems and ADHD in their epidemiological study.

Tannock and Schachtar (1996) argue that the association between ADHD and communication problems is greater than could be expected by chance and that therefore their development is linked. They also state that children with ADHD are more likely to have communication difficulties than vice versa. So there may be something about ADHD which makes the development of a communication problem more likely.

ragmatic language deficits could both be due to a common
xecutive function. Executive function is a higher order
ess required for controlling attention, regulating resource
-ordinating processing, and planning, organising, monitoring
ng behaviour. Working memory is crucial to executive functioning, d communicative competence, because in working memory input
from various sources, for example auditory and visual, is integrated with
linguistic and social knowledge to produce an appropriate response. Young
people with ADHD seem to have deficits in working memory (Siegel and
Ryan 1989). The core features of ADHD (inattention, impulsiveness and
over-activity) seem to be due to problems with self-regulation and these are
related to difficulties with executive function (Barkley 1994). Poor topic
maintenance, interrupting and excessive talkativeness, which are common in
children with ADHD, are also related to executive function deficits.

The disruption of executive function in ADHD could also impair other
self-regulatory behaviours, such as the development of 'private' speech (or
internal language), and this could explain why so many children with ADHD
also have problems using internal language and developing narratives.
Therefore, it is possible that, for some children, emotional and behavioural
problems and communication difficulties stem from the same cognitive
deficit.

Common causes of behavioural and communication problems

As the previous sections have shown, there is limited evidence for simple
direct links between emotional and behavioural problems and communication difficulties. There are, however, various factors which could be responsible for both kinds of impairment. Genetic predisposition, adverse environmental factors, interaction and attachment problems, child abuse and learning
difficulties are all potential causes of both emotional/behavioural and communication difficulties.

Genetic predisposition

There appears to be a genetic component in the development of some
emotional and behavioural problems and communication difficulties. The
genetic influence on internalising disorders, for example, seems to be quite
strong (Rende *et al.* 1993). For other psychiatric difficulties, genetic factors
lead to a susceptibility to develop the disorder, but only in the presence of

other environmental factors, which could be the case in depression, schizophrenia and ADHD. It is also thought that genetic factors are relevant in some cases of communication difficulty (Felsenfeld and Plomin 1997). However, there is no evidence yet for the same genes being responsible for both emotional and behavioural problems and communication difficulties.

Environmental factors

Unfortunately, many children have to deal with adversity of various kinds from birth. The following are all possible risk factors for developing language and emotional and behavioural difficulties: cognitive impairment, sensory impairment (particularly hearing disability as a risk factor for communication problems), central nervous system dysfunction (such as cerebral palsy), adverse family conditions, low socio-economic status, psychosocial stress, parental (particularly maternal) mental illness, perinatal complications, brain injury and premature birth. The more of these factors that are present, the higher the likelihood of impaired language and emotional and behavioural development (Baltaxe and Simmons 1988a). An example of how these factors can interact is in children who 'fail to thrive'; they are often found to have oromotor dysfunction (that is, abnormal development of the muscles of the mouth), which is also a risk factor for speech problems (Mathieson et al. 1989).

When considering the factors in the background of children with psychiatric difficulties, Frisk (1999) found that these young people experienced developmental delays, difficulties such as dyslexia (which is closely related to verbal language difficulties), cognitive deficits such as attention deficits, slow complex reaction time and adverse social conditions.

The influence of adverse social conditions should not be underestimated. It is still the case that many children come from backgrounds where there is considerable environmental stress, a lack of stability, family discord, inadequate nutrition and limited access to proper medical care, which can be detrimental to many areas of development, including language (Wells 1981). As Holman, at a conference in 1998, said, 'Poverty undermines parenting.' Children from families with unskilled occupations are about three times as likely to have a mental health problem as children from professional families. Pollution, particularly lead poisoning, could also be a factor in the co-occurrence of emotional and behavioural difficulties and communication problems. Children born to mothers who overuse alcohol may be born with foetal alcohol syndrome, which includes distinctive behaviour such as impulsivity, disinhibition, and being demanding of affection and physical contact. It also includes difficulties with understanding and using language, which tend to persist (Abkarian 1992).

Bilingualism per se is not a risk factor for communication or behavioural problems. In typically developing children, bilingualism confers considerable advantages in terms of an awareness of language as an abstract entity. However, learning an additional language is most successful when the child can engage in frequent conversations with native speakers, so any child who has difficulty engaging with others will be at a disadvantage. Therefore, children who are having problems with developing communication skills or who have developmental delays or neurological difficulty may experience difficulty when learning additional languages, which could result in emotional and behavioural difficulties. Bilingualism may be a relevant factor in some cases of selective mutism, for example.

Disruption of early interactions

It takes two to interact and sometimes early interactions cannot be responsive because the parent and infant are not equally responsive or communicative. Some parents find it easier to interact with their offspring and to interpret their communicative intents than others. There is no formal training to be a parent, so parents are reliant on their own experiences of being parented, as well as the examples around them, and these may not always be good models. Stresses or impairments in either the parent or child can impair their ability to interact responsively.

The classic example of this is depressed mothers who are unable to be responsive to their infants. Mothers who are depressed seem to encourage a style of rapid attention switching in their children, because they tend to change topic rapidly. In addition, their children are generally under-stimulated, which affects various areas of development. Children whose mothers were depressed when they were less than a year old are more likely to have learning difficulties, and unsurprisingly language delay is also associated with maternal depression.

Children with emotional and behavioural difficulties tend not to elicit as many positive interactions from their caregivers as their peers and this can lead on to language delays. Behavioural difficulties tend to elicit directive, less responsive interactions; such children may not be sensitive to social interactions and therefore have fewer conversations with other children, resulting in less language 'input'. Similarly, children with communication difficulties may find social interaction stressful and unrewarding and thereby become depressed and despondent and interact even less. The adults in these unrewarding exchanges also suffer frustration and can become discouraged.

There may also be differences in the way people from different socio-economic groups interact with their children. According to Hart and Risley (1995) children in working class families hear fewer words and learn fewer.

Variety in temperament and the presence of impairments also affect the way babies are able to interact. Babies and children who are inattentive, impulsive and distractible may be more difficult to interact with. Those who have communication difficulties will similarly be less responsive and may eventually receive less input because of this. Visually impaired infants are unable to establish mutual gaze and shared attention through eye contact, so although many children with visual impairments develop language well, some have delayed or disordered communication skills. To gain an optimal outcome, parents may have to be especially responsive and eager to interact with their child in the face of little reaction. If there are lots of children who require attention, this obviously puts an extra strain on the parents. For example, being a twin adds a risk of language delay, perhaps because of having to share attention or perhaps because of the additional stress a multiple birth places on parents.

Barden et al. (1989) studied children with craniofacial abnormalities (such as cleft palate) and their carers. They found that these children received less nurturing than their siblings did, although their carers were unaware that this was happening. Such craniofacial abnormalities may also lead to attachment difficulties (Knutson and Sullivan 1993), which, through impairing responsive interactions, could compound communication problems.

It is uncertain whether the linguistic model provided for a child can create language problems, but difficulties with responsive interactions, or meshing, have been implicated in some communication problems (Schaffer 1989). Where interactions become unresponsive, attachment difficulties occur.

Attachment difficulties

Ainsworth et al. (1978) proposed three types of mother–child attachment (though these can be applied to whoever is the principal caregiver). There are caregivers who respond to children in ways that are predictable and comforting, leading to secure attachments. This has been described as 'an affectionate bond between two individuals that endures though time and space and serves to join them emotionally' (Fahlberg 1981, p.7).

There are also caregivers whose responses are predictable and distressing, and there are those whose responses are unpredictable and inconsistent. These respectively lead to anxious-avoidant and anxious-ambivalent types of attachment in children. Other types of attachment have also been identified, including insecure disorganised attachment and, rarely, children who are unattached. Unattached children are unable to give or receive affection at all and they can be destructive to themselves and others.

An attachment disorder develops when a child's need for safety, security and trust are either not met or ignored. As a result, children may become inhibited, hypervigilant or ambivalent in the presence of their carers, or they may be over-familiar with strangers and unselective in their choice of attachment figures. As children grow older they don't necessarily have to be near a parent to feel safe, but their attachment to them is symbolised and remembered, so if securely attached they are gradually able to become more independent and self-confident. Unfortunately, the same is true of an insecure attachment; it is remembered and affects future interactions. Thus, early attachment difficulties can affect a child's ability to form attachments as they grow older and reach adulthood. Insecure attachment has negative effects on a child's emotional and communication development, as well as their ability to learn.

Anxious-avoidant children learn that expressing their feelings leads to uncomfortable outcomes – for example, parental anger, rejection or unavailability. Therefore, such children will try not to express their feelings; to them, only thinking is meaningful. These children may be hostile and socially isolated. Anxious-ambivalent children learn that expressing their feelings has no predictable outcome, so for them neither thinking nor emotions are particularly meaningful. The inconsistency they experience means that information may be lost or falsified and this can result in illogical thinking and confused narratives in children and adolescents. These children may be over-dependent and lack confidence.

According to Crittenden (1995), attachment disorders pose a risk to mental functioning and language development, because they lead to distortions of memory as uncomfortable emotions are inhibited. Memory, and the language used to encode it, can be affected when memories of specific events are distorted by omitted, misinterpreted and forgotten information (Loftus and Hoffman 1989). Also, if one's caregiver is inconsistent, generalisations become difficult and this can affect the ability to learn. Memories of very emotional events tend to be the most long-lasting. It may protect a child in the future if very emotional incidents are stored in long-term memory, but these emotional kinds of memory may become overly significant in children whose memory for other events is distorted by attachment difficulties.

Children who have emotional and behavioural difficulties are twice as likely to come from discordant families than children with no such difficulties. As children grow up, language is the medium through which their relationship with caregivers is mediated and thought about. When a child cannot get reliable information about the future linguistically, because what parents say can be unreliable, they may learn to distrust language. They may instead attend excessively to their caregivers' behaviour and they are therefore less free to engage in the exploration which is crucial for their development.

There is some evidence which shows that language development in abused children is most severely impaired where attachment is affected. According to Law and Conway (1989), who carried out a review of the literature on child abuse and language development, 'neglect' has the most significant effect on a child's language development, and the clearest effects occur where the neglect affects the parent–child attachment. This then becomes a reinforcing negative spiral.

Another type of insecure attachment is known as 'disorganised'. This pattern is common in children who are abused or neglected and it occurs when the parent is either frightened or frightening. The child is in an impossible position because they experience two incompatible drives, to approach (attach) and to avoid because of fear, and this can be devastating for a child's development. These children may seem depressed, irrational and disorganised.

Child abuse and neglect

When parent–child interaction breaks down to the extent that child abuse or neglect occurs, there are negative effects on many areas of a child's development. Abuse and neglect have a negative effect on a child's general development, health and growth, including their emotional, cognitive and linguistic progress. The emotional effects include the development of a negative self-image, difficulty managing emotions and behaviour problems. Child abuse also seems to have a negative effect on health and educational outcomes (Adcock and White 1998; Jones and Ramchandani 1999). Abused infants and their carers are more likely to ignore each other than other parents and children. Abusive and neglectful mothers interact with their children less; they are unlikely to play with or talk to them and more likely to ignore what they say. The language they do use tends to be more controlling. This would indicate a breakdown in meshing and this could contribute to delayed language development in the children (Allen and Wasserman 1985).

Abused children are not good at recognising emotions in others and they are unlikely to express their own emotions verbally. They tend to just use language to get things done. They find it difficult to consider contextual cues when interpreting emotions and they have particular problems interpreting complex and conflicting emotions, so they are likely to think that others are being aggressive towards them even when they are not (Pollak *et al.* 2000). They are also at a disadvantage in learning how to manage their own behaviour because they do not have the appropriate emotional vocabulary. Such children have difficulty making and maintaining relationships and learning. As their language skills tend to be concrete they have difficulty with the abstract language necessary for literacy. There could also be longer-term effects, since a history of abuse and neglect is common in adults who have psychiatric difficulties.

Abused and neglected children seem to be particularly at risk for communication difficulties (Coster and Cicchetti 1993). They have more comprehension difficulties than their peers and their expressive language is also affected. They use more repetitions in their speech, they tend to have smaller vocabularies and use shorter sentences. Also, abused and neglected children are less likely to talk about what they are doing and less likely to ask for information. They also use fewer internal state words, such as emotion vocabulary.

It has been difficult to identify the effects of maltreatment on children because abuse and neglect have not always been clearly defined in research and they are not mutually exclusive. Also, if abuse or neglect affects or results from early problems with responsive interactions, the effects may not be obvious immediately, as language does not emerge till later. However, neglect seems to be the most damaging to communication development, probably because it deprives the child of a responsive relationship. Language development may be more affected than some other areas of development because it is more environmentally sensitive.

However, it is not always clear which is cause and effect when it comes to abuse and neglect and developmental difficulties. Children who already have neurological and developmental difficulties, such as language impairment, and who are also subject to social stressors, are more likely to suffer child abuse. Child abuse and neglect can be seen as the result of many factors, one of which is the child's propensity to health and developmental problems, including communication difficulties and the stress this creates. It seems likely that having a child with any kind of disability is a chronic stressor for carers and a potential attachment disrupter. Clearly, some parents have the internal and external resources to cope with a child who has difficulties and some do not. Knutson and Sullivan (1993) have argued that many handicapping conditions could also be due to abuse, so it is often difficult to determine which came first.

McCauley and Swisher (1987) found that speech and language problems in a child may lead to neglect, and this can lead on to emotional and behavioural difficulties. Sadly, children with disabilities of all kinds are more likely to suffer abuse and neglect. Disability makes abuse easier, especially in children who are communicatively impaired. Their communication difficulties also make it harder to identify that abuse has taken place and such children may not be seen as competent witnesses.

Some physical abuse involves specific injuries resulting in communication difficulties; for example, vocal cord damage can be caused by attempted strangulation (Myer and Fitton 1988), or head injuries may lead to cerebral palsy (Bax 1983). Neurological changes may also result from abuse and neglect. It seems likely that there would also be emotional repercussions from such appalling injuries.

Learning difficulties

Learning disabilities or general neuro-developmental delay may be a common cause of behavioural and language problems. Large numbers of children with serious emotional problems also have learning difficulties (Fristad et al. 1992), probably three times as many as other children (Meltzer et al. 2000). Also, as a child's academic problems increase, so do his or her behavioural difficulties (Gallico 1986). Similarly, the behavioural outcome is likely to be worse if language impairment is associated with low IQ (Silva et al. 1984). Some language delays due to neuro-developmental delay may resolve with maturity and this could be part of the reason why rates of communication and behavioural difficulties decline with age (Goodyer 2000).

Specific deficits in cognitive processing could underlie some behavioural and language difficulties and explain why these are often closely associated. Cognitive processing is defined as the skills required for problem-solving and abstract reasoning. These skills include attention, processing speed, and memory, and deficits in these areas could also impair behavioural and language functioning (Rock, Fessler and Church 1997). Executive dysfunction has been linked to learning disabilities, antisocial behaviour and attention deficit disorder, as well as language problems. Students with learning disabilities and emotional problems have also been found to have deficits in executive function, social interaction and attention (Bricklin and Gallico 1984). Bradshaw (2002) argues that neuro-developmental disorders such as ADHD, Tourette's and autism, amongst others, are due to dysfunction of the frontal lobes, which is also the origin of executive function, so it is likely that with further research more neurological links between communication and behavioural difficulties may become apparent.

Some argue that the relationship between emotional and behavioural difficulties and communication difficulties is due to problems with complex cognitive functioning or neurological immaturity, not language functioning (Gilliam and De Mesquita 2000), though in other large-scale studies, patterns of social and behavioural problems were not associated with cognitive ability, or gender (Botting and Conti-Ramsden 2000). Learning disability cannot be the entire explanation for the association between language impairment and emotional and behavioural problems, since not all children with emotional and behavioural problems and communication disorders also have learning disabilities. Language and intelligence are separate. People may suffer cerebro-vascular accidents (strokes) that impair their ability to communicate in various ways but not other cognitive abilities. Similarly, young people who have communication difficulties do not necessarily have learning difficulties. Also, most IQ tests tend to be loaded with language, so communication-impaired children may score poorly because they are language-impaired rather than because of limited intelligence.

Developmental effects

To add to the complication, the links between emotional and behavioural difficulties and communication problems change over time. In a child's early years the foundations of emotional/moral/learning behaviour, self-concept and self-control are laid down. As each of these develop, or fail to, they can affect the development of other areas. Children with one developmental difficulty are at high risk for others. Preschool communication-impaired children are likely to have immature and overactive behaviour. Attention difficulties and toilet training are also often problematic. After starting school they may go on to develop internalising disorders, particularly anxiety. Later on into adolescence externalising behaviour problems may occur, particularly if there have been literacy difficulties. It is not clear whether the type of emotional and behaviour problems change in response to the communication difficulties a child experiences, or because the occurrence of psychiatric problems changes with age in all children.

Children and young people also respond to their difficulties in different ways. They may make accommodations to problems, and later on there may be attempts to overcome or mask them. The relationship between emotional and communicative function also changes over time because integrations with other intact areas may be necessary for further development, and when these can't occur further problems arise, for example literacy and social interaction difficulties.

Conclusion

There are likely to be various links between communication difficulties and emotional and behavioural problems. No one link is relevant to all children with emotional and behavioural problems and communication difficulties. There are children with communication problems and no behaviour difficulties and vice versa; similarly, there are children who live in adversity and who do not develop emotional or communication problems. The relationship between communication and emotional and behavioural difficulties seems to be complex and transactional. It depends upon factors within the children, including their resilience to negative factors around them, the caregivers' response and the environment. For some children, multiple factors seem to conspire against typical development.

Although attachment disruption may be a significant factor, it is important not to ignore the wider context, particularly where that includes psychosocial disadvantage. The mediating factor in the development of some communication and emotional and behavioural problems seems to be changes in thinking, either in executive function or theory of mind, which have direct effects on interactions, thereby influencing further learning and social adjustment. The frustration and social isolation which can result from communication difficulties should not be underestimated.

More subtle measures of communication skills and behaviour will be necessary to identify any relationships between the two more clearly. There is also a great need for more research in this area. It is important for practitioners to consider both the communication skills and the emotional and behavioural difficulties a child may experience. A step towards this is proposed by Goodyer (2000), who suggests a classification of communication problems, including non-linguistic features, as follows:

- Simple developmental disorder: personal and social impairment together with one or more speech, motor or behavioural symptoms. These difficulties are likely to improve with time.

- Mixed developmental disorder: including language, motor (including ADHD) and literacy disorders. This may be the most common type and there may not be a good outcome, depending on severity.

- Complex developmental disorder: a mixed developmental disorder with additional difficulty with the social use of language.

- Semantic pragmatic disorder: this consists of a particular difficulty with the social use of language. Behavioural difficulties may result.

This type of definition, as well as multi-axial schemes which gather information about other significant risk factors impinging on a child, may help us understand more about how emotional and behavioural and communication difficulties come to be associated, but a great deal more research is necessary before we know which are the most useful classifications.

CHAPTER 3

Undetected Communication Problems, Their Impact and Why They are Undetected

In the last two chapters I have argued that communication and emotional development are interlinked, so it is unsurprising that disorders of communication and emotional and behavioural difficulties tend to occur together. More than half of young people who have emotional and behavioural difficulties of various kinds have communication difficulties and a similar number of young people with communication difficulties also have behavioural or emotional problems. However, these links have not always been recognised and are still not obvious to everyone working with children who have emotional and behavioural difficulties.

More seriously, there is a growing body of evidence that shows that many children with emotional and behavioural problems have communication difficulties which have *not been detected*. The consequences of this are serious for the young people involved. They seem to be at greater risk of communication difficulties than other young people, and these difficulties have serious negative effects on behaviour and emotional development, social interaction and learning. If a young person has undetected communication difficulties, they are at risk of potential misdiagnosis and inappropriate interventions. Consequently, the issue of previously undetected communication problems has considerable implications for anyone working with children who have emotional and behavioural difficulties.

How many children have communication difficulties?

In order to appreciate the scale of communication difficulties amongst children with emotional and behavioural problems, it is important to consider how often communication difficulties occur in general. However, this is not straightforward. It is difficult to determine how many children in the general

61

population have communication difficulties because various different definitions of communication impairment are used in research and indeed the nature of communication problems seems to change over time. It is relatively easy to identify preschoolers who are not talking as much as their peers, but as children mature their language deficits may appear primarily as difficulties with social relationships or with learning. Also, young people may be reluctant to talk or interact, so any communication difficulties may not be apparent without specific investigations. Communication problems also become more or less obvious depending on the academic and social demands of the environment. A young person may cope well at home, where the language is contextualised and often predictable, but they may have great difficulty in school, where the language is abstract and often referring to things beyond their experience.

Despite these confounding factors, various studies have found similar incidences of communication difficulties in preschool children. There also seems to be a consensus that the number of children with language difficulties declines towards school age. Whitehurst and Fischel (1994) concluded that 9 to 17 per cent of two-year-olds had language impairments, 3 to 8 per cent still had such problems by three years of age, and by five only 1 to 3 per cent seemed to be language impaired. Similarly, in a survey of 30 six-month-old children in Cambridgeshire, 7 per cent were found to have language difficulties (Burden et al. 1996). Tomblin et al. (1997) sampled over seven thousand children in the rural mid-west of the United States and found a prevalence of developmental language delay of 7.4 per cent. Law et al. (2000a) found a figure of 5.95 per cent for speech and language delay in their review of the literature on the prevalence of such difficulties.

Although there is little evidence about the prevalence of communication difficulties in school-aged children, there is evidence that language impairments can persist into adolescence and beyond. Beitchman et al. (1996) followed the development of a group of five-year-old children with communication problems and 70 per cent of them still had difficulties at the age of 12.

Some of the studies quoted here may underestimate the incidence of communication problems because they do not all include children who have difficulty with the use of language. Differing experimental designs, including variation in the communication difficulties included, could account for some of the variation in estimates of the prevalence of communication difficulties, but even accounting for these, it seems likely that less than 10 per cent of all children have communication difficulties.

In contrast, the incidence of communication problems in children who also have emotional and behavioural difficulties seems to be markedly higher; estimates range from 60 per cent (Cohen *et al.* 1993) to 90 per cent according to Camarata *et al.* (1988). Benner, Nelson and Epstein, who reviewed the literature on language deficits in children with emotional and behavioural difficulties, concluded that approximately three quarters of children with EBD also had language deficits and 'the rate of co-morbidity between language deficits and EBD tends to be stable or to increase over time' (2002, p.43). Also, about half of children with communication difficulties seem to have emotional and behavioural difficulties. Burgess and Bransby (1990) found that 16 of 17 pupils in a unit for children with emotional and behavioural difficulties had communication problems. In my experience of working with children with these problems in the care of the local authority, I have found that the majority of such young people also have difficulties with communication and that most of these difficulties have not been previously detected (Cross 1999).

Unsuspected communication problems in children with emotional and behavioural difficulties

So children who have emotional and behavioural problems are very likely to also have communication difficulties, far more likely than children and young people without emotional and behavioural problems. This is very significant for those young people, but more seriously there is also evidence that these communication difficulties often go undetected and unaddressed.

Researchers have consistently found that a third or more of children referred for help with emotional and behavioural problems have unsuspected communication difficulties (Cohen and Lipsett 1991; Cohen *et al.* 1993, 1998a, 1998b; Giddan, Milling and Campbell 1996; Jones and Chesson 2000; Kotsopoulos and Boodoosingh 1987). Most recently, Schultheis (2001) analysed the language and behaviour of 129 preschoolers and found that children with some behaviour problems were likely to have communication disorders which were undetected.

Studies of children with emotional and behavioural problems in special education have also found that there is a high prevalence of language difficulties, often undetected (Burgess and Bransby 1990). Law and Sivyer (2003) also found undetected communication difficulties in children with emotional and behavioural difficulties who had been excluded from school.

Therefore, studies of children with emotional and behavioural difficulties of various ages, in differing contexts and using different assessments, have all found that many such children have undetected communication problems. There are indications that the prevalence of undetected communication difficulties may be even higher than these studies suggest, as they did not all assess for pragmatic or social communication problems, despite evidence that these problems were found to be particularly prevalent amongst behaviourally disordered children (Baltaxe and Simmons 1988b). Therefore, children with emotional and behavioural problems seem to be at much greater risk of communication impairment than children in the general population and it is likely that their communication difficulties will not be recognised as such.

Furthermore, the prevalence of approximately 30 per cent of unsuspected communication problems remains consistent into adolescence in the psychiatric population, whereas the prevalence of communication difficulties seems to decline amongst other children as they become older (Cohen 1992). Toppelberg (2000) reviewed the previous ten years of research into communication difficulties in children and concluded that, although language difficulties are high risk factors for psychiatric problems and have implications for evaluation, therapy and research, they are often undiagnosed.

The significance of undetected communication problems

Does it matter that children and young people have communication difficulties? Is it likely to make any difference to them whether these difficulties are detected or not? The resounding answer is yes, communication difficulties have a negative impact on the ability to socialise and learn, and undetected communication problems can expose children and young people to misdiagnosis and inappropriate interventions, as well as potentially exacerbating their emotional and behavioural difficulties.

In comparison to other children, the language used by children with emotional and behavioural disorders is less informative and effective, and it does not mature with age (Rosenthal and Simeonsson 1991). It is also characterised by shorter utterances, poor topic maintenance, inappropriate responses and inappropriate speech style (McDonough 1989). They are also likely to have difficulty understanding language. Essentially, their communication skills are ineffective and this can negatively affect many areas of their development.

Behavioural and emotional consequences

It has long been recognised that expressive language difficulties are often associated with anxiety. This is something we all experience to some degree when we can't explain ourselves or we have a difficult presentation to make, but Trapp and Evan (1960) found that children who had unintelligible speech had heightened anxiety levels that corresponded to the severity of their pronunciation difficulty. So the presence of communication difficulties could increase anxiety in a child who already has emotional and behavioural problems.

Communication difficulties could also contribute to behaviour problems, or may be sometimes interpreted as behaviour problems. Cohen and Lipsett (1991) found that the children who had unrecognised communication problems (38 per cent of their sample) were 'rated by their mothers as more delinquent and by their teachers as exhibiting more psychopathology' (p.376).

They concluded that it was the 'invisible' nature of some communication problems (particularly difficulty understanding language) which led people to perceive these children as more behaviourally problematic. Such children fail to understand instructions, get frustrated, and inappropriate behaviour may result. This is exacerbated by the fact that they may not be able to show that they have misunderstood, either verbally or non-verbally, or indeed they may not realise that they have misunderstood. Such skills develop at about eight years of age in most children (Bonitatibus 1988), but may not be present even in teenage language-impaired children. In some cases simply the diagnosis of a communication difficulty improved behaviour because those talking to the child were able to accommodate to their difficulties and misunderstandings were not seen as defiance.

Children who have communication problems are not easy to parent. Paul and James (1990) discovered that parents of children whose language development was delayed found them more difficult to manage than children whose language was developing normally. This is because a large part of the 'management' of young children is done verbally. It is necessary for a child to understand a request in order to co-operate with it; and indeed toddlers have been found to be compliant with adult requests that they understand (Kaler and Kopp 1990). Young people with undetected communication problems may be unable to follow routines, understand instructions or interact appropriately at school or at home, and they often receive negative attention for this, despite the fact that they don't purposely 'behave badly'. So it seems likely that children who have communication difficulties can be seen as 'difficult' and this is likely to be compounded if the communication difficulties are not recognised.

For the language-impaired child, there can be considerable frustration because they are not able to express their needs or make themselves understood. Caulfield (1989) investigated a 'frustration model' of the relationship between language delay and behaviour problems. She found evidence for this in that situations that were communicatively difficult generated misbehaviour. Further evidence for the frustration link in younger children comes from Laplante, Zelazo and Kearsley (1991), who trained parents to manage their children's oppositional behaviour and found that, as the misbehaviour decreased, vocabulary and verbal interaction increased in comparison with controls.

Communication is not just about getting one's needs met, it is also important for the expression and regulation of emotional states. Children's abilities to understand and talk about emotions are related to their behaviour. Cook, Greenberg and Kusche (1994) found that children who had more behavioural problems were less able to talk about their emotional experiences and were less able to identify emotional cues (such as facial expression and tone of voice) in others. Children with behaviour difficulties have problems understanding emotion. Difficulty understanding emotion vocabulary accounts for some of this. There is also some evidence that learning to label emotions may help to manage them (Hesse and Cicchetti 1982). So unidentified communication difficulties could not only contribute to emotional and behavioural problems, but they could also hamper the development of further emotional growth.

Self-perception is another important factor in emotional development. Many children with communication difficulties are aware only of failure and other people's anger and frustration. As they grow older, they begin to recognise the differences between themselves and others. By the age of nine (Ackerman 1982) most children understand and can use plays on words and jokes as a means of interaction, but these are difficult to understand for language-impaired children; as their self-awareness grows, they realise that they do not have the tools to interact successfully and to have fun with others.

Sigafoos (2000) argues that delayed communication development may contribute to the development of inappropriate behaviour in developmentally delayed children. Lynham and Henry (2001) have demonstrated that antisocial behaviour is related to impairments of language skills and self-control functions (executive function). In addition, it has long been known that children who have persistent conduct disorders are very likely to have verbal deficits (Moffit and Lynham 1994). Aggressive children have also been reported to use fewer verbal assertions and more non-verbal direct action solutions to problems than control subjects (Bloomquist *et al.* 1997). This is likely to be because language skills are essential in the development of self-control. Initially, language helps us to internalise the input from parents and others which helps us realise what is safe; young children often learn words like 'hot' or 'burn' early on, as their parents try to explain why they shouldn't touch fires etc. Later, language skills can be used 'in our heads' (as inner speech) to enable us to consider the consequences of our actions and decide what to do in response to a threat or emotional upset. If language skills are lacking, a violent response might be the only recourse in a perceived threatening situation.

Gualtieri *et al.* (1983) concluded that 'disorders of the development of language are likely to be central to the development of human personality. Understanding and correcting deficiencies of language can improve behaviour and help a child resolve at least some of his emotional dilemmas' (p.169).

EXAMPLE 1

> Shaun is a good example of this; his comprehension difficulties meant that most lessons were unintelligible to him. He could do quite well in practical lessons when he could watch the other students, but when he had to listen to the teacher for any length of time, it didn't make sense to him and he got very bored. His favourite way of amusing himself was to pull a rubber apart and flick pieces at other students. This was not acceptable to anyone else in the class, although he made some of his peers laugh. After his communication difficulties were identified, efforts were made to encourage him to ask for clarification and he was taught some of the unfamiliar vocabulary and concepts used in class. He was then more likely to engage in the lesson and his behaviour improved.

Social consequences

Language impairments have a negative effect on a child's behaviour, but also on his or her ability to interact with others; indeed, the two are closely linked. Verbal reasoning has an important part to play in social interaction as well as in self-regulation because of inner speech. Inner speech mediates between intention and action (Kendall and Braswell 1985). Inner speech also enables us to reflect on how others behave and why: 'Language skills facilitate executive control and metacognitive processing by providing a means for self-reflection, verbal mediation, response inhibition and behavioural direction' (Gallagher 1999, p.5).

The pragmatic aspect of language – that is, the use of language to interact socially – is dependent on the development of cognitive skills like executive function as well as on linguistic, social and affective development (Baltaxe and Simmons 1988a; Barkley 1997). Fundamental interaction skills, such as understanding social cues, social problem-solving and identifying and labelling emotions, as well as understanding their potential consequences, are all language-facilitated (Kusche, Cook and Greenberg 1993). When there is conflict, most children learn to give an opinion, suggest alternatives and negotiate compromise. These alternatives are just not available to children who have communication difficulties and who have difficulty 'reading' and understanding how others feel. Similarly, such children may misinterpret teasing as an attack and 'hit back' (Rinaldi 1996).

As a result of their interaction difficulties, children with language impairment tend to be rated by parents and teachers as having poorer social competence (Beitchman et al. 1996). An example of this is Cohen's study (Cohen et al. 1998b). This found that children with language impairments (whether or not these had been identified) had more difficulty with social cognitive processing than children who had normally developing language. Such social cognitive deficits mean that language-impaired children have difficulty identifying the feelings of those involved in a conflict, negotiating, and realising when a conflict has been resolved. Children that Cohen et al. (1998b) assessed who had normally developing language, and who had been referred for a psychiatric assessment, also had social cognition deficits, but not to the extent of the language-impaired children. Therefore, limitations on language development can severely inhibit the development of appropriate interaction skills and may worsen behaviour problems – surely a significant fact to consider in children who already have emotional and behavioural difficulties.

Communication difficulties can also lead to social isolation. Failure to understand others and to express your own wants and desires is seen as socially inappropriate and other children are not always tolerant of such deficiencies. This is underlined in work by Loucks and Gallagher (1988), who reported that language-impaired children's behaviour led to disputes more often than that of their peers. Guralnick *et al.* (1995) also observed that children with communication disorders had fewer positive social interactions and spoke with peers less often during non-play activities. When children have social problem-solving deficits, they are less assertive, less co-operative, and have less self-control. This makes it harder for them to make and maintain friendships. It may also seem to others that they don't want friends. However, the value of friendships should not be underestimated. Among other things, friends help children develop appropriate behaviour, provide support and assist the development of self-esteem and moral behaviour. Fujiki, Brinton and Todd (1996) found that children with specific language impairment had poorer social skills, fewer peer relationships and were less satisfied with these relationships than their peers. Asher and Gazelle (1999) suggest that children with language disorders are particularly at risk of loneliness because of their peer relationship problems. Life-long social isolation can also result from such interaction difficulties.

EXAMPLE 2

> Part of Jacob's social communication problems was that he did not know how to ask to join in others' games. He resorted to pushing girls and trying to steal the ball from the boys at play times, in attempts to engage the other children. Once his communication problems had been identified, social communication group work and circle time sessions were used to teach him appropriate ways to join a conversation, as well as the nature of co-operative games. Subsequently, he could play with others rather than just annoy them.

Educational consequences

Longitudinal studies have shown that children with specific language impairment have persistent linguistic, social and educational impairments over many years (Baker and Cantwell 1987; Rissman, Curtiss and Tallal 1990). The main educational consequence of communication problems is poor literacy skills; such difficulties seem to be linked to deficits in processing speech sounds, which often occur in children with communication impairments. For literacy to develop, a child has to identify the speech sounds which make up words, then understand how these are represented by letters and letter combinations. Even young people who have intelligible speech may have difficulty with hearing the difference between speech sounds, segmenting words into sounds and blending speech sounds. Children with communication difficulties often also have difficulty with auditory memory so they may not be able to remember speech sounds or instructions long enough to process them. Good vocabulary skills are also important for reading, so language-impaired children are often at a disadvantage because even if they can 'decode' the letters into sounds, they may not recognise the resulting word. Therefore, children with emotional and behavioural problems, as well as having language deficits, may be particularly at risk of literacy failure. Children with emotional and behavioural difficulties often have major difficulties with literacy and numeracy (Farrell, Critchley and Mills 1999), and most pupils in EBD schools have difficulty with literacy (Ofsted 1999). Ironically, reading failure also seems to exacerbate problem behaviour (McGee *et al.* 1986), and it is well known that many children with conduct disorders often have undetected reading problems. Literacy difficulties also seem to be a risk factor for social difficulties, unemployment and criminality.

If a young person has difficulty understanding language this will affect all areas of learning; 'all education takes place through the medium of language' (Halliday 1991, p.1). Language is the medium of instruction; children are expected to listen for about 60 per cent of the time in primary or elementary education (Dunkin and Biddle 1974), and this increases as pupils get older. If a young person has particular difficulty with auditory processing, as many language-impaired young people do, learning in a mostly auditory environment is very difficult and stressful and many give up.

Some argue that children with language deficits have difficulty with reading primarily because they have problems with comprehension. Findings which show that mathematic ability may also be impaired in children with language difficulties fit in with the suggestion that difficulties understanding linguistic concepts affect learning in all areas. More worryingly, these difficulties with maths and literacy may persist into adulthood. Often language-impaired children find it difficult to generalise concepts and they are often seen as rigid thinkers. It may be so difficult to understand the concept of 'take away' as it relates to maths, that it is just too much to accept that 'minus' and 'subtract' are the same thing, and that a chicken curry can also be a 'take away'.

Berk and Landau (1993) observed that children with language difficulties relied on externalised private speech; in other words, they needed to think out loud because they had not yet developed inner speech. A child or young person who cannot work quietly may have difficulty in class; such behaviour is not necessarily acceptable, either to classmates, the teacher or the pupil him- or herself, especially as he or she gets older.

The likelihood is that children and young people who have undetected communication difficulties may be at additional risk of educational underachievement. This could further lower self-esteem, as children with specific language impairment see themselves more negatively in terms of school achievement, social acceptance, and behaviour as they grow older. This negative self-image may be even more relevant to young people whose communication difficulties are not recognised (Jerome *et al.* 2002). It takes a very strong individual to persist when one constantly makes mistakes and where learning takes a great deal of effort.

Children with verbal deficits may be unable to engage with lessons and therefore find school dull and irrelevant. Many would argue that unpleasant school experiences are likely to lead to inappropriate behaviour (Cloward and Ohlin 1960). Primary education is becoming increasingly collaborative, and children who have communication difficulties find the necessary negotiation and co-operation particularly difficult (Brinton, Fujiki and Higbee 1998). Since excluded children have been shown to have undetected communication difficulties (Law and Sivyer 2003), it may be the case that attention to the communication difficulties of children who are about to be excluded, as well as specialist behavioural support, could reduce the number of exclusions from school.

EXAMPLE 3

> Anthony was 13 years old when he started at our school. He found it hard to learn in a group setting of five to six students, disrupting lessons with constant interruptions and persistent changes in topic. This resulted in Anthony receiving individual tuition outside of the classroom for much of his first term. Language and communication difficulties had not been previously identified.
>
> A speech and language therapist assessed Anthony after a couple of months at a special school. Assessment showed that he had significant language and communication problems, including difficulties under-standing what was said to him. The results of the assessment were shared with Anthony. It was suggested that one of the reasons he was getting into trouble in class, with his interruptions and changes of subject, might be because there would be less chance of misunderstanding what was being

said if he wasted time or took control of the topic. This was a revelation to Anthony. He looked as if a 100-watt light bulb had just been switched on in his head. 'So that's what's wrong with me!' he exclaimed.

Over the next few weeks, Anthony was back in class for the majority of his lessons and there was a significant reduction in his interruptions and disruptive behaviours. What was startling about this dramatic turn-around was that he had barely started his speech and language therapy course. The changes in his behaviour appeared to relate to 'just knowing' that he had language and communication problems. His unidentified language difficulties had exacerbated existing behaviour and educational problems.

Potential misdiagnosis and inappropriate interventions

If a young person has communication difficulties it will be difficult for them to understand what is expected of them, to justify their actions, to respond appropriately and to interact with others without discord. If one is not aware that a child or young person has communication difficulties, such behaviours can seem like oppositional, or at least uncooperative, behaviour.

When there are disputes or misbehaviour, children and young people are often required to explain themselves. However, children with communication difficulties, especially if they impair narrative structure, are more likely to describe events rather than to explain what is happening (Williams 1993), and they may not be able to produce cohesive and coherent answers to specific questions. Consequently, young people with undetected communication problems may be in trouble for behaving inappropriately or not doing as they are told, then considered to be defiant for not justifying their behaviour.

As a consequence, children and young people who have undetected communication difficulties are likely to have their behaviour misunderstood. Additionally, adults may interact with them at an inappropriate linguistic level. Often the language adults use is too complex and abstract for them to understand. I once heard someone say to a group of children with emotional, behavioural and communication difficulties, after a disruption in class, 'Who precisely precipitated that palaver?'; needless to say, the palaver continued. Behaviour and behaviour problems are dealt with through language and often the child's linguistic ability is overestimated. Some young children may not be able to understand conditional phrases, so the sentence 'If you do that again x will happen' might sound like 'Do that again'; the consequences of their action, presented in this way, won't make any sense to them. (This is aside from the fact that they may not have the reasoning or self-control skills to respond to this kind of injunction.) Similarly, Burgess and Bransby (1990) found that the behavioural modification techniques being used with the children in their study (who had unsuspected language problems) made considerable use of the language of emotion and verbal reasoning, both of which were likely to prove difficult for children with communication problems. It had been assumed that the children's lack of co-operation was entirely due to oppositional behaviour, rather than a lack of understanding. If inappropriate behaviour serves a child's communication needs and an acceptable (verbal) alternative is not available, then behaviour modification, which is aimed at just reducing unacceptable behaviour, is unlikely to work. This is dealing with the symptom, not the cause.

If a young person has undetected communication difficulties and they are unfortunate enough to be abused or neglected, resulting in legal action, they can be further disadvantaged. A valid interview cannot be carried out without an understanding of the young person's language abilities. Sadly, I am aware of several cases where a conviction was not possible because the young people involved did not have the communication skills to cope with the legal system. Given that many young people with communication problems have difficulty with narratives, there are major implications for their involvement in legal proceedings, particularly as witnesses. Their communication difficulties should be borne in mind and questioning modified accordingly. In my experience, when their linguistic limitations are pointed out, the young people may be deemed incompetent witnesses.

Another potential misunderstanding is in underestimating the potential of young people with undetected communication problems. If a child has difficulty interacting, their behaviour may be judged as 'immature', resulting in an underestimate of the child's true ability or potential. Behaviours indicative of communication problems may also be mistakenly attributed to psychological problems. Redmond and Rice (1998) investigated children with specific language impairment (as well as normal intellectual functioning) and emotional and behavioural problems as they started school. They found evidence to support the idea that these children did not really have emotional difficulties but that their 'difficult' behaviours were simply adjustments related to their limited language skills. Teachers expect children to have mastered basic social skills before they start school and may project 'social immaturity judgements' onto children with speech and language limitations (Rice, Wilcox and Hadley 1992). So, for at least some children, anxious and inhibited behaviour may not be indicative of psychopathology at all, but indicative of communication problems.

Gualtieri *et al.* (1983) argue that children with communication difficulties can display behaviour which could be interpreted as symptomatic of a psychiatric disorder when faced with language they cannot interpret. They may, for example, become agitated and disorganised. More seriously, there are disruptions in the flow of discourse in children who have psychiatric difficulties, whether or not they have additional communication problems, so there is the potential to confuse narrative difficulties with serious psychiatric illness. A young person with difficulties with the use of language, perhaps difficulty staying on topic, can be difficult and even bizarre to converse with, but they are not necessarily emotionally disturbed. Quite rightly, mental health professionals focus on a child's behaviour and emotional state; however, their assessment will be carried out using language, and differentiation may depend on responses to questions posed, so it is important to also consider the language skills of young people who have emotional and behavioural difficulties. If they have difficulty understanding language they may well give 'inappropriate' answers to questions. Limited expressive skills will also affect results.

Gualtieri *et al.* (1983) also questioned the validity of using language-based psychological or psychiatric assessments on children who may be language-impaired. They observed that, in situations where the language demands were appropriate to the child's level of functioning, very different behaviours were apparent than in situations where language demands exceeded the child's capacity; when the linguistic demands of a situation are beyond the abilities of the child or young person, inappropriate behaviour may result. If a differential diagnosis is based on a child's responses to questions, an inappropriate diagnosis could be reached. Many young people with difficulty understanding language will not comment if they do not understand the questions, perhaps because they do not know how to, perhaps because they are used to adults not making much sense or perhaps because they are too embarrassed to admit to their difficulties.

Another relevant factor in the misinterpretation of communication problems as behaviour difficulties is that assessments of emotional and behavioural status often have items on them which could relate to language difficulties alone rather than behaviour problems. For example, in the 'Internalizing and Attention Problem Syndrome Scales' of the Achenbach Child Behaviour Checklist (1991), there are items such as 'refuses to talk' and 'has difficulty following directions' (Redmond and Rice 1998). Therefore, according to this checklist, a child with communication problems would automatically be considered as also having behaviour difficulties.

Why are communication difficulties undetected?

Perhaps the main reason why communication deficits are undetected is that they are not necessarily expected or sought out; but there are also other reasons. Tomblin *et al.* (1997) commented that children with developmental language disorder were likely to be under-diagnosed. Only a third of the children who took part in Tomblin *et al.*'s study had been previously diagnosed as having a language disorder. It may be that language difficulties are generally under-diagnosed. This also applies to other difficulties children have; for example, there is some evidence that psychiatric difficulties are often undetected in children in the care of the local authority.

Language deficits may be subtle

Cohen *et al.* (1993) found that, overall, those children with undetected communication problems had less severe language impairments than those whose communication difficulties had already been identified. They also suggested that children with undetected communication problems were those with more subtle deficits, such as receptive difficulties. It is easy to recognise a child with unintelligible speech or one who uses sparse and immature sentences. However, it is difficult to identify comprehension difficulties; a child may not respond appropriately because they do not understand, but such a response might also be due to a lack of interest or co-operation. Young people who do not always understand spoken language may be unaware of this problem or unable to indicate when they don't understand.

Many undetected communication difficulties are 'higher level'; that is, the sound system, grammar and vocabulary seem to be age-appropriate but there are difficulties with the social use of language, which cannot be identified by simple formal assessments. Such communication problems may only be identified if they are sought out. Difficulties with narrative structure or discourse can often only be detected by a specific investigation, as they may only appear in 'demand' settings rather than during informal conversation (Stark and Tallal 1988).

Cohen *et al.* (1998a) also found that children with unsuspected language difficulties had milder academic impairments than children whose communication problems had been detected. Academic difficulties often alert those working with a child to the fact that they may have communication problems. If a child is coping quite well at school then language difficulties may not be suspected or mild academic problems may be seen as being due to an overall learning difficulty rather than a specific impairment.

Behaviour difficulties may be more obvious than communication problems

Communication difficulties may be overlooked if a child also has more salient disruptive behaviour (Cohen *et al.* 1998a), especially if language deficits are subtle. Cohen *et al.* (1993) found that boys with unsuspected communication problems were more likely to have externalising behaviour difficulties, for example Conduct Disorder. Although there does seem to be a link between communication problems and aggressive behaviour, it is often the aggressive behaviour which gets the urgent attention. Interventions to address aggressive behaviour may seem to be a priority, but these are unlikely to succeed if verbal impairments are not considered, particularly if these interventions are language-based. As has been argued, communication difficulties can also be misinterpreted as behaviour difficulties.

Psychosocial disadvantage

Cohen *et al.* (1998a) found that the children in their studies with undetected communication problems had mothers with less education than those children with normally developing language. It may also be the case that language disabilities have a genetic basis (Rapin 1996), so perhaps some parents of children with unsuspected language problems have communication difficulties themselves. Tomblin *et al.* (1997) found higher concentrations of children with language disorders in lower socio-economic groups. In the context of poverty and limited education, it is unsurprising that subtle difficulties such as communication problems are not detected or that help is not sought for them. However, psychosocial disadvantage is not relevant to all children with communication difficulties or all children with emotional and behavioural difficulties.

Race may also be relevant here; Tomblin *et al.* (1997) argue that lower parental education accounts for the high incidence of developmental language disorder in racial/cultural minorities. The research into children with unsuspected communication difficulties and emotional and behavioural problems is mostly based on children who speak English, and only English;

there is a need for research to investigate the links between communication difficulties and emotional and behavioural difficulties in children and young people learning more than one language.

Language impairments change in nature

Another factor which makes communication problems difficult to define and identify is that they change over time. Children who are seen as language-impaired before they start school are often seen as learning disabled when they begin school (Bashir *et al.* 1983). Furthermore, as children reach adolescence the links between language and thinking become more apparent. As a child grows older, language deficits impact on reasoning, organisation of knowledge and conceptualisation (Wiig 1995), so language deficits can easily be confused with general learning difficulties. It is also very difficult to know what a child's language skills ought to be like at any given age as there is considerable variation within the normal range (Wells 1986).

Lack of awareness and training

Another reason why communication difficulties may not be identified is that language development, identifying language disorders and recognising the significance of communication problems are rarely part of the training received by social workers, foster carers or teachers. In addition, there is some evidence that parents and medical professionals tend to overestimate the ability of children to understand language (Sattler, Feldman and Bonahan 1985), such that it is the subtle deficits which often go undetected. Toppelberg (2000) suggests that child and adolescent psychiatrists need an understanding of language development and disorder in order to make the appropriate referrals. This is also true of any professional working with children with emotional and behavioural problems.

Conclusion and implications

Communication problems have far-reaching negative effects on important aspects of a child's development. Camarata *et al.* (1988) and Benasich *et al.* (1993) conclude that speech and language assessment should be a routine part of the management programme for children with emotional and behaviour disorders. This is particularly important as there is also some evidence of a worsening of language difficulties if they remain unsuspected (Cohen *et al.*

1998a). There is also evidence that just the diagnosis of a communication problem can improve a child's behaviour, as it changes the way other people interact with him or her (Cohen *et al.* 1998a). Some parents involved in Cohen *et al.*'s study reported that the assessment had helped them to understand their children's behaviour and that they had more positive interactions with them. Therefore identification in itself can be valuable.

There is also a need for increased awareness of language development and impairment amongst professionals working with children with emotional and behavioural problems so that they can accommodate to a child's communication difficulties (Giddan *et al.* 1996). If children have emotional, behavioural and communication problems it is essential to understand their language capabilities in order to help them resolve other difficulties.

Identification is important but it is only the beginning. Clearly the next step is to do something about these communication difficulties. Adults can modify their communication in order to make interaction easier and young people can be taught many of the communication skills they need.

CHAPTER 4

Unidentified and Unmet Communication Needs in Young People in 'Public Care'

Introduction

Historically, children and young people in public care have not necessarily had their health and educational needs recognised or met and this includes communication difficulties. Government initiatives in the UK such as *Quality Protects* (Department of Health 1998) seek to improve the situation. There are some hopeful signs, but it remains to be seen whether there will be significant improvements in health and education services for children and young people, who often need more from such services than children cared for by their own parents. Historically, despite governmental attempts to improve the situation for children in need, there tends to be a variable compliance with these laws.

Although children in public care may have greater needs for special educational services and more health needs than other children, there is a lack of special education provision for them, and they seem to have problems accessing the health care that they need. Children who are in public care may also suffer because of a lack of co-ordination between the agencies which are responsible for different areas of their care. Adults are often seen as the real consumers, even of children's services such as health and education (Alderson 1995), so children without consistent adult advocates (the turnover of social workers can be as rapid as changes of placement and school) are clearly at a disadvantage when it comes to accessing the services they require.

In the context of such unmet needs, it is not surprising that communication problems in children in public care also go undetected. Communication difficulties are a prime example of problems which impact on many areas of a child's development, but which do not fit neatly into any service delivery model. Speech and language therapy is mostly provided by the health service, so to that extent communication problems are seen as health needs. However, the consequences of communication problems are often educational, so communication difficulties should also be seen as special educational needs. This division leads to confusion about responsibilities for helping children with communication difficulties, and as a result communication difficulties often remain unrecognised and therefore young people suffer the negative emotional, social and educational consequences outlined in the previous chapter. Even those young people whose communication difficulties are recognised may not get help because of shortages of trained staff.

Children and young people in 'public care'

In every society, there are children and young people who are in need of extra support in order to flourish. One way to describe these children and young people is 'in need'. A definition of 'in need' was formalised in the UK by the Children Act (Department of Health 1991a). The term 'in need' refers to children who are unlikely to achieve or maintain a good standard of health or development, or whose health and development will be impaired, if special services are not provided for them. It also includes children and young people who are disabled. Children and young people who have emotional, behavioural and communication difficulties are in need of extra help and support and co-ordinated service provision is necessary to meet those needs. Such children form a substantial minority of the population. The number of children known to social services because they are in some way 'in need' is estimated at about four hundred thousand in the UK (Department of Health/Department for Education and Employment/Home Office 2000). Legislation often formalises the duty of the government to safeguard and promote the welfare of vulnerable children. There is an emphasis on directing additional resources to these children as well as a duty on all agencies to co-operate in order to meet these children's needs. In the USA there is a federal entitlement to early intervention services, and service co-ordination is mandatory.

Some children and young people 'in need' are 'looked after'; this is also known as being in 'public' or 'statutory' care – that is, they are in the formal care of the local authority or the state. This can happen either by virtue of a court order or they are accommodated on a voluntary basis.

Care Orders are made where social services can show that a child or young person is suffering, or is likely to suffer, 'significant harm' if left in their parents' care, either because the level of care is inadequate or because they are beyond parental control. In 2002 about 59,000 children were in statutory care in the UK. Due to the decline in residential care the majority of children in public care are now fostered. In the USA in March 1998 520,000 children were in foster care (US Department of Health and Social Services, Administration for Children and Families). These children have often been affected by parental substance abuse, abuse or neglect, domestic violence, poor housing or frequent moves, poverty or homelessness, and they may also have special needs or disabilities. They often come from families with few resources or little support.

The unmet health needs of children in public care

Given their circumstances, which often include a hostile perinatal environment, exposure to drugs, parental stress, malnutrition, neglect or abuse, it is not surprising that children in public care have higher rates of emotional and behavioural difficulties, physical disabilities, general health difficulties and developmental delays. Such children may also have found it difficult to access services because of language or cultural barriers. Children in foster care have been found to have poor health generally (Chernoff et al. 1994) and their health needs tend not to be met (Risley-Curtiss et al. 1996). Reasons cited for this, both in the UK and the USA, are problems with funding, planning, waiting lists and poor co-ordination and communication between services. For many children, a placement in foster care can lead to improvements in health (White and Benedict 1986), but not for all.

Schneiderman et al. (1998) point out that the presence of developmental delays in children in foster care may not only result in poor academic achievement, but also secondary emotional and behavioural problems. Other researchers (Thompson and Fuhr 1992; Urquiza et al. 1994) have also found high levels of behavioural disorders in children in 'out of home' care. Indeed, the most prevalent problems amongst children in public care are probably emotional and behavioural ones (McIntyre and Keesler 1986). Garland et al. (1996) found that just over half of the foster children in their study (in California) had received some kind of mental health services within six months of being removed from their homes. This is approximately ten times the uptake of such services by other children. However, Dubowitz et al. (1990) found that only 12 per cent of children with emotional and behavioural problems were receiving treatment for these difficulties.

McCann et al. (1996) investigated adolescents in the UK care system and found that they had particularly high levels of psychiatric disorders when compared with their peers who still lived with their families. Most worryingly, there were many whose psychiatric problems had gone undetected. This is despite the fact that others (Bamford and Wolkind 1988) have found that their risk of psychiatric problems is higher than that of any other easily identifiable group. This is in the context of very few specifically adolescent health services, though such young people have a specific set of health needs.

Identifying and trying to improve any medical problems are important since, apart from any other consideration, children with developmental delays and/or behavioural problems tend to have a longer length of placement with foster families (Horowitz, Simms and Farrington 1994). Foster carers need training in identifying, and support in dealing with, the health care needs of the children in their care (Halfon and Simms 1994), especially as the burden of caring for a child who has complex medical needs, without specialist support, is likely to be a factor in the breakdown of foster placements. The importance of supporting the foster family is underlined by research which shows that the relationship children form with their foster carers is probably the most important element in the promotion of their health (Ruff, Blank and Barnett 1990).

Interestingly, hearing losses, which will impact on communication, are also often undetected in children with emotional and behavioural difficulties. Giddan *et al.* (1996) found that in a sample of children in a psychiatric in-patient unit, 17 per cent of subjects failed a pure tone hearing screen and 25 per cent failed tympanometry (which assesses middle ear function). In this study, 60 per cent of the children also had a speech and language deficit.

Children who are asylum seekers are children in need, and they have specific and sometimes serious health needs. They may not have had primary immunisation and they may have been exposed to serious illnesses. Mental health issues are very relevant given the circumstances which have led them to flee their own country, the stressful and dangerous journey they have undertaken and the problems when they arrive in a host country. Added to this, there are few interpretation services available. Any communication difficulties are therefore very unlikely to be identified or helped.

Possible solutions

Part of the reason for all these children's poor health is the inadequate care that they had before they were in public care. However, their problems seem to be compounded by frequent changes of foster placement. Another factor, relevant to this, is the lack of historical information about development and medical matters. Medical examinations may be carried out by doctors other than the child's general practitioner, who therefore do not have access to their medical records. Centralised medical records would help in this process, or, as Butler and Payne (1997) suggest, designated doctors for children in the care of the local authority. Butler and Payne found that only a quarter of children looked after by a local authority attended statutory medical examinations. So, legislation alone does not encourage those who are responsible for children in public care to consider the child's health as important. Young people themselves have expressed dissatisfaction with the system of medical examinations, which they often find to be impersonal, stigmatising and unhelpful. In addition to which, these examinations do not necessarily address young people's health needs.

Simms and Halfon (1994) recommend early medical and psychosocial screening for all children in foster care. They also stress the importance of subsequent access to the treatment found to be necessary. Horowitz (2000) suggests that specialised clinics for foster children are necessary to identify all their problems. Furthermore, on-going case management is also seen as crucial for children with such complex needs.

The *Quality Protects* programme in the UK is attempting to address the needs of looked-after children. There is now a requirement for all children entering local authority care to have an assessment of their health needs and a plan of how these needs will be met. This plan should be regularly reviewed. This is a move towards a more holistic approach, as this health assessment should now include physical and mental health and health promotion. Another important strand in this is that the needs and wishes of the young people should be considered and that their informed consent should be obtained. Assessments should also take into account the children's ages and developmental levels and particular circumstances. For children under five, the review will be at least every six months.

Another initiative is the Joint Assessment Framework (Department of Health/Department for Education and Employment/Home Office 2000) which will provide a common framework for the assessment of children in need. The aim of this framework is to link the work of local councils and health services around children in need; this should make information sharing easier, with due regard to consent and confidentiality. Unfortunately there is little mention of communication difficulties in the first draft of this assessment. There are also plans for health records to be 'fast tracked' if children move out of the area, so that their health care can continue uninterrupted. There should also be designated staff responsible for the health of children in public care within health and social services. This can include doctors, nurses and school nurses. Carers are also identified as having a key role in the health of a child and they are responsible for promoting a healthy lifestyle within the family (see the National Minimum Standards, Fostering Services Regulations – Department of Health 2002).

The Children's National Service Framework (see www.doh.gov.uk/nsf/children/), another new UK programme, aims to 'improve the lives and health of children and young people…through the development of effective, evidence based and needs led services'. The development of children's trusts, which will provide integrated support systems for children and young people, will help to provide integrated care to those who need it. Within this programme there is a focus on meeting the needs of children in public care, and it is hoped that the barriers to achieving this, such as a lack of skilled staff, will be overcome.

The educational needs of children in public care: low achievement and special educational needs

Children in public care tend not to do well educationally in comparison to their peers (Heath, Colton and Aldgate 1989; HM Inspectors of Schools and the Social Work Services Inspectorate 2001; Utting 1997). Biehal *et al.* (1995), in a study of young people leaving care, found that 75 per cent of them had no qualifications. To some extent, young people in public care do not succeed in school because of factors in their lives before they were 'looked after' by the local authority (Department of Health 1991b). In particular, children who are in public care because of suspected abuse or neglect have lower scores of educational attainment than children who had come into care for other reasons (Aldgate *et al.* 1993). This is not surprising, given the considerable amount of evidence about the negative effects on many areas of a child's development of abuse and neglect.

When children come into public care, initially the focus is to find them a safe and stable environment. Stable placements have to be a first priority since an uncertain environment may be damaging to a child's ability to form attachments (Department of Health and Social Security 1985; Department of Health 1991b). It is also understandable that children's physical care is very important, as many of these children have been neglected and/or abused before coming into care; there have also been children who have been abused while in care. However, the high priority given to a child's physical needs while in public care is another reason why special educational needs, including communication difficulties, may have been overlooked. This is not to say that it is not important for young people to have time to fit into a new placement, and indeed they may not be able to cope with school until they have had time to settle in, but appropriate educational placement must be considered as part of the care they receive.

Children may need help to recover from negative life experiences, and education can be part of this process in its development of confidence and self-esteem. Education can have a therapeutic value for children, leading to a sense of normalisation, particularly when young people are able to make measurable progress and form positive relationships with staff and students. Success in education is crucial in determining adult lifestyle and social inclusion (Jackson and Martin 1998). Therefore, appropriate education should not be overlooked as a means of raising self-esteem. However, education may not have been valued enough in the past.

Education is crucially important to the quality of adult life and, if their education is disrupted, children who are in public care are further disadvantaged. However, once in public care, a child's education may continue to be disrupted by numerous unplanned moves, and consequently they may be out of school for long periods. Children taken in to public care may also have to change school if placements can only be found away from their home area. Starting a new school is an additional stress for any child. Apart from the negative impact this has on education, relationships can be lost and consequently there are fewer adults to act as advocates for the child's needs, or friends to help support the young person. If they move during an academic year it can often be difficult to join their peer group and this can result in bullying, further adding to low self-esteem. Children from ethnic minorities are over-represented in the population of children in public care and they may experience racism once separated from their peers. Such moves are another reason why young people in public care may not gain qualifications; to achieve these they need to spend several years in the same school in order to adequately cover the required syllabus. Such moves also make it difficult to monitor a student's progress.

Children in public care may also not progress so well academically because they have special educational needs. Sawyer and Dubowitz (1994) found that children in kinship care (fostered within the extended family) seemed to have more special educational needs and language and cognitive difficulties than their peers. However, the special educational needs of children in public care may not be addressed at all. It takes time for a school to recognise and understand a child's needs, so frequent unplanned moves impair this process. Hayden (1997), in a paper on exclusion from primary school, states that children who have been or who are 'looked after' by the local authority are over-represented in cases of exclusion, as are children with special educational needs. Indeed, she argues that children who are excluded from school are actually children with special educational needs or children otherwise 'in need'. So, part of the reason for the poor academic achievement of children in public care may be that, not only do their special educational needs go unrecognised, but their more obvious behavioural problems lead them to be excluded as well. Parsons (1994) found that the majority of children with emotional and behavioural difficulties in his study were referred for assessment of their special educational needs. However, many were excluded before any conclusion could be reached. It may also be the case that being brought up in a foster or residential home predisposes children to inattention and hyperactivity, which can lead to difficulties with behaving appropriately at school (Roy, Rutter and Pickles 2000).

Further evidence that children in foster care may have unrecognised special educational needs comes from Goerge et al. (1992) in a study in Illinois. They found that six times as many foster children received special educational services than had been previously recognised. They had to employ special techniques to use information from two incompatible databases in order to identify these children. They also found that these children were on average older than other children who had special educational needs. Screening procedures may only be in place for younger children, so if special needs are not identified at an early age they are unlikely to be detected later, or it may be deemed 'too late to do anything about it'. When there is no one to 'fight' for the children's needs, as most parents would, then their special educational needs may not be met.

Another reason that children in public care don't succeed educationally may be because there have been low expectations of them. It seems likely that among children in public care there is a spread of ability, as in any other group of children, and often those who could achieve well academically are disadvantaged because their potential is underestimated. Good behaviour in school may be seen as progress enough, although this does not necessarily mean that the young people are achieving their potential; it is important not to confuse sympathy with lowered expectations. Children in public care may also fail because their special needs are not recognised or met, rather than because of previous life experiences. Therefore, it is important to investigate the causes, rather than make assumptions, if a child or young person in public care is failing educationally.

Lack of special educational provision

Pupil Referral Units were set up in the UK to help children excluded from school to return to mainstream education, but in practice they are rarely able to meet these children's special educational needs and the children who attend them are unlikely to return to mainstream schools (Morris 1996).

If children in public care have emotional and behavioural difficulties – and they often do – there may not be the resources to help. Schools for students with emotional and behavioural difficulties are rare. Visser and Cole (1996) identified 20 local education authorities which did not have any provision for children with emotional and behavioural problems, and very few pupils at the schools which do exist ever reintegrate into mainstream schools (Farrell and Tsakalidou 1999). When special schools were first inspected by Ofsted (Office for Standards in Education) in 1985/86, 73 per cent of them were found to be unsatisfactory or poor; however, there has been a marked improvement since then, and by 1998 only 17 per cent were unsatisfactory (see Office for Standards in Education 1999). Such schools often function with very little help from other agencies and there is a great need for the development of integrated services to meet the complex needs of these students. 'Few schools reported that they were actively assisted by social workers and only a few reported regular or extensive contact' (Ofsted 1999). Educational psychologists are often seen as a valuable resource for such schools, although they usually have little time to offer EBD schools.

Special educational needs may be identified and addressed within mainstream schools, but if these are emotional and behavioural in nature, schools may not have the resources or training to help. In striving for inclusion for children with emotional and behavioural difficulties, it is necessary for all staff to be trained and to share the philosophy of inclusion, but this is not necessarily the case (Hamil and Boyd 2001). For inclusion to work, teachers need to believe in the 'ecosystemic' view of behaviour, that only part of it is due to the individual's internal state and the rest of it influenced by the environment, which can be changed. Although LEAs (Local Education Authorities) in the UK are now required to develop Behavioural Support Plans, which should include a policy for managing behaviour in mainstream schools as well as EBD (emotional and behavioural difficulty) units, these are very variable and do not always include services to support mainstream staff. Some head teachers of EBD schools felt that improved practices in mainstream schools could reduce the number of EBD referrals (Ofsted 1999). Simple measures such as increasing the amount of positive feedback to pupils have been shown to improve behaviour, whether or not the pupils have emotional and behavioural difficulties (Swinson and Cording 2002; Swinson and Melling 1995).

Mainstream schools are increasingly responsible for their own (often reduced) budgets, in an increasingly competitive environment where the achievements or otherwise of their pupils are made public. A cynical view is that children with emotional difficulties, including those in public care, are too expensive in terms of time and resources and a cheaper alternative may be to exclude them from school. Consequently (until recently) there has been an increase in exclusions from schools in the UK.

Even if a young person in public care is not actually excluded, their special educational needs may not be met.

EXAMPLE 4

> Billy has some learning difficulties and a statement of special educational needs. The local school has a place but will not offer it to him as they know he will not have his needs met without support. They cannot get funding as the funding for the year has already been agreed and Billy's money would have gone to his old school. Meanwhile, Billy is offered part-time tuition at home from someone who is not aware of, or trained to help him with, his particular learning difficulties.

Educational welfare officers are often valuable advocates for excluded children and they also have a role in making referrals to specialist agencies when necessary. However, this begs the question of whether it is obvious that such referrals are necessary. It may not always be obvious when a young person has special needs, as has been argued with regard to undetected communication difficulties.

If there is no appropriate educational provision, children who are excluded from school may get some sort of home tuition, which is not the same as individualised teaching to address any special educational needs. It is variable in amount – sometimes no more than two hours a day – and may be provided by unqualified staff. Some excluded pupils get no tuition at all. Clearly, in this situation children miss out on the social and interactive learning available in school, as well as on adequate amounts of good teaching to address any special needs they may have.

Ofsted commented, 'The likely negative consequences on educational standards and on future opportunities in adult working life which are created by a long-term, part-time educational placement cannot be over-estimated.' Many young people in secure accommodation have been in public care and have suffered significant disruption in their education. It seems unlikely that this is a coincidence. Children 'looked after' by the local authority seem very likely to have special educational needs which go unrecognised and unmet.

The way forward

Research focusing on the needs of children in public care has demonstrated significant gaps in provision and achievement. This has led to specific government responses such as the UK *Quality Protects* initiative *The Education of Children and Young People in Public Care* (Department for Education and Skills/Department of Health 2000), a programme of social services reforms including achievement targets and 'Guidance on the Education of Children and Young People in Public Care'. Local authorities are now required to provide children in public care with a personal education plan (PEP) within 20 days of entering care or joining a new school, and to appoint designated teachers to liaise with social services and act as an advocate for these children. The PEP should ensure access to services and support, highlight special needs, establish clear goals and act as a record of achievement. It should also include targets relating to academic attainment, personal achievements and behavioural competence, and responsibilities for carrying out the plan should be identified. Unfortunately, if needs are identified which the school cannot address, such as communication difficulties, these needs continue to go unmet.

All local authorities were required to produce an action plan of reform and by July 2001 50 per cent of children in local authority care should have achieved at least one GCSE pass at age 16. Not all pupils achieved this but most were making good progress (Ofsted 2001). There were also aims to reduce truancy and exclusions of children in public care which appear to be taking effect (Ofsted 2001).

An Ofsted report in 2001 recommended the promotion of greater understanding between social services and education, including joint training. Multi-agency working is seen as a duty and necessity. Social workers and foster carers have an important role in improving the educational attainment of children in their care.

The social worker has responsibility for informing the school and local education authority when a child is taken into public care, starting the PEP in partnership with the school and ensuring the relevant professionals participate. The PEP is seen as useful by schools as it gives more information than an individual education plan (Ofsted 2001). The designated teacher ensures that the PEP is agreed and that the carers receive relevant information; they also co-ordinate the school's part in the review process. The carers are expected to value and prioritise education, including helping with homework and attending school events. They are also encouraged to play an active part in planning and liaison, and to encourage and celebrate success.

In this collaborative process effective communication is important; ignorance of significant factors at home or at school could lead to inappropriate management. However, issues of confidentiality often impede this. Carers have a huge responsibility when it comes to encouraging literacy and supporting homework, especially when the young person has difficulty in these areas. They also have an important role in helping to manage unacceptable behaviour. Sometimes difficult behaviour is only present in one setting, either in the foster home or at school, which can make understanding and managing it more difficult. In order to help the child it is vital that carers and school staff understand the demands of each context and work together to support the young person in behaving appropriately in each.

It is also important to have both the right foster placement and school and that the two liaise well. A stable placement is one of the most important factors leading to a good educational outcome for foster children. A successful outcome is also more likely if long periods out of school are avoided. If children are well placed in school, they are better protected and offend less. Conversely, problems in education are a major factor in the breakdown of foster placements.

It has also been recognised in *Quality Protects* that older pupils in public care will have special needs. Older, disaffected young people should have access to a realistic and flexible curriculum, including work-related learning and careers advice. They should also have a personal adviser for training to independence.

It may be the case that, despite supportive foster carers and help with special educational needs, children in local authority care still don't progress educationally. Heath, Colton and Aldgate (1994) found that even children in long-term, settled placements did not 'escape from disadvantage'. They conclude that, as a history of abuse and neglect has such lasting effects, only exceptional educational inputs are likely to overcome this.

Collecting data

Centralised information about the needs of a child in public care and their previous assessments, as well as how many such young people there are, is vital, both for the progress of the individual and for the development of services. It is also useful for the monitoring and evaluation of such services. Shared or centralised information is particularly important when children change placement, school and GP and records may be lost or difficult to transfer. Such records are even more valuable when it is not possible to get a thorough case history and developmental information from parents.

Although required to collect data on children in public care by the *Quality Protects* initiative, few local authorities were able to do this in the initial stages, though many of them had plans to do so. The least information was available on children in need, children with mental health difficulties and ethnicity. Information about health was usually more readily available than that about education (Department of Health 1999). Efforts are being made to collect information and make it transferable, though a great deal of work needs to be done to even make databases compatible. Local authorities are making efforts to develop useful databases but the information gathered can't yet be used to assess the progress of individual children (Ofsted 2001). Further work is necessary to gather and share information between social services and education in order to allow for appropriate planning and monitoring of children's progress. Education authorities and health authorities do not necessarily have mutually agreed data sets, so this can make planning very difficult, as can the fact that local education authorities and health trusts rarely have common boundaries (Law *et al.* 2000b). Some would argue that administrative solutions are not enough (Horowitz 2000), though it seems likely that they would help.

Training

Skill shortages have been reported in relation to meeting the demands of *Quality Protects*, particularly when working with children with complex difficulties. Gaps in skills, especially in the area of child development and special needs, have also been identified in child care and education (Local Government Management Board 1997). In an attempt to improve child care, there is a move towards developing training to improve competency and to increase working together of services. There is also an aim 'to raise the quality of child care so that it is as close as possible to the care provided by loving and responsible parents (Training Organisation for the Personal and Social Services 1999).

Interdisciplinary training seems to be an important element when it comes to helping children with complex needs. Training for all professionals is necessary in health, emotional and education issues. Academia is divided into subject areas but children are not. Practitioners need training from people from different disciplines and there needs to be a clearer link between theory and practice. All too often, practitioners are expected to make this leap for themselves during their first 'qualified' years. Training alongside different disciplines not only helps in understanding their theoretical viewpoint, but also the practical difficulties they face. Professionals need to be aware of the terminology and the legal and practical contexts in which others work.

The communication needs of looked-after children

Assessment of children and young people coming into public care is, among other things, meant to be rooted in child development, so what about communication skills? Is their development understood and are they carefully assessed? The Looking After Children, Assessment and Action Records (Department of Health 1995) consider seven dimensions: health, education, identity, family and social relationships, social presentation, emotional and behavioural development, and self-care skills. Although it could be argued that communication skills are vital for development in many, if not all, of these areas, they are barely mentioned. These forms have not helped to identify communication difficulties in children in public care in my experience (Cross 2001). Unfortunately, the special educational needs procedure doesn't necessarily identify communication problems either (Burgess and Bransby 1990), so even if a child has a statement of special educational need, they may have undetected communication problems.

EXAMPLE 5

> Ewan was 12 years old when I met him. His foster carers referred him for a speech and language therapy assessment very soon after he was placed. His Statement of Special Educational Needs said 'his communication skills are good, he listens well and can express himself clearly'. Very little

other information was available about him. However, assessment showed that he had problems with understanding and constructing language as well as difficulty using language appropriately in a social context. He had difficulty with the abstract language used in class and he had difficulty negotiating with his peers. He also had a very limited vocabulary, so although he could converse quite well on a topic of his choice, when asked to give specific answers or explanations in class he was unable to respond and often got distressed by this.

Some researchers see language acquisition as essentially a preschool task (Masten and Coatsworth 1998). However, language development is probably a lifelong process and a 'developmental task', which, if not achieved successfully in the preschool years, will impede other such tasks in middle childhood and adolescence.

There is mounting evidence of the link between emotional and behavioural problems and communication difficulties and indeed of undetected communication problems in looked-after children (Cross 1999, 2001). Over a number of years, I and my colleagues have identified a startling number of young people in public care who have significant communication difficulties which had not previously been recognised, and it seems likely that children in public care in other contexts also have unrecognised communication difficulties.

EXAMPLE 6

Alex is 14 and as soon as his foster carers met him they realised that he was unusual. Nothing in his records gave any clues about why some of his behaviour and communication was so difficult to understand. After a speech and language therapy assessment which gathered information in various ways and in various contexts (see the next chapter for details), it became clear that he has severe specific social communication difficulties and it was later confirmed that he has Asperger's syndrome. Having recognised the nature of his difficulties, it was possible for all who work with Alex to address them.

Even if communication difficulties are identified in children in public care, it is likely that these children will find it difficult to access appropriate services, essentially because there are hardly any. There are very few speech and language therapists working with children in public care or with children with emotional and behavioural difficulties, though guidance suggests this should be increased (Law *et al.* 2000b). Similarly, there are limited speech and language therapy services to secondary aged students and those in mainstream schools. There is also debate about whether health or education authorities should fund speech and language therapy for school-aged children (McCartney 1999), which adds to the difficulty in accessing services.

Involving young people in decision-making about their care and the services they need is increasingly seen as vital. This is necessary even when children have severe communication difficulties (Ward 1997); however, it will be more difficult if these young people have undetected communication problems. Unidentified communication difficulties no doubt contribute to the social, emotional and educational difficulties long suffered by children in public care. Communication difficulties are 'needs', as defined by the Children Act, which are not necessarily being met for children in public care. It is hoped that new initiatives will improve the detection of communication problems in children in public care, but there is still a great deal of work to be done in this area.

Conclusion

It remains to be seen whether the quality of services for children in public care will improve as a result of recent reforms in the UK. Ofsted (2001) reported that 'The raised awareness of the needs of children in public care through the *Quality Protects* initiative and through the issuing of the "Guidance on the Education of Children and Young People in Public Care" is having a positive effect on provision in schools, and on expectations and outcomes for the children' (3.4, p.7). However, there is a lack of consistency across the country. Continuity of care and a co-ordinated treatment approach is an aim still to be met, but worth striving for, and there are reports of better joint working between education and social services. It is hoped that adequate resources will be available to support these worthy initiatives, and that integrated working for the benefit of young people and their families will result.

Communicating with children effectively and enabling them to express their needs and views will only be effective if their communication strengths and weaknesses are understood and allowed for. This can be especially relevant to looked-after children who may have to appear in court. Undetected communication difficulties in children in public care is a serious and ongoing problem.

CHAPTER 5

The Identification and Assessment
of Communication Difficulties

Introduction

In this chapter there is a discussion about the nature of communication problems as well as the merits of various methods of identifying and assessing them. Given the negative effects of communication difficulties and their often 'invisible' nature, it is important to identify and assess them. Beitchman *et al.* (1996) found that children who had speech and language difficulties identified at age five were likely to have poorer linguistic and academic outcomes at age 12 than their peers. They concluded: 'These findings reveal the urgent need for early intervention among children with pervasive speech/language impairment' (p.804).

Effective remediation can only occur if communication difficulties are recognised and if there is a good assessment of 'the problem'. Also, inappropriate behaviour is a form of communication, so it is crucial to be able to identify the communication function of that behaviour, or what the young person is trying to 'say'. An assessment of communication skills can help with this and enable the development of more acceptable forms of communication. Although it is accepted that it is important to identify young people who have difficulty learning language and to intervene to help them, there is no consensus about how best to detect young people with communication difficulties. The type of assessment used will be influenced by the reason for carrying out the assessment. Assessment may take place for research purposes, but mostly it occurs in order to identify those eligible for services and in order to guide interventions. Law and Conway (1989) also suggest that an ongoing assessment of the communication skills of children in public care might be a 'barometer of the success of the placement'.

What are communication problems and how are they identified?

There is no simple answer to this, because adequate communication is hard to define. Language is a moving target; not only is it continually changing and being added to, but it varies greatly according to the socio-economic, minority and educational status of those using it. Individuals also vary the language they use according to where they are and who they're talking to. Consequently, identifying communication problems is not a simple matter.

Language pathology is the study of communication difficulties and it is a relatively new field. There has been considerable debate over the definition of 'communication difficulties' and 'specific language impairment'. Indeed 'specific language impairment' and 'communication difficulties' are different things, the former occurring in the absence of other difficulties. The technical use of everyday words such as speech, language and communication probably adds to the difficulties that exist in identifying or even discussing communication problems. Suffice to say that communication impairment encompasses a wide range of disabilities ranging from difficulty understanding language to problems with fluency, all of which can co-occur. The causes of many communication problems are unclear (Lewis, Cox and Bynard 1993). So it is not possible to determine which 'symptoms' are most significant in identifying communication difficulties. However, there have been suggestions that problems with sound processing underlie many communication difficulties (Dollaghan and Campbell 1998). There is also some evidence that links 'semantic-pragmatic' type difficulties (which include problems with using vocabulary and social communication) with right hemisphere dysfunction, and 'phonological-syntactic' problems (or difficulty with organising sound and words into appropriative sequences) with left hemisphere dysfunction (Sheilds et al. 1996), but this kind of evidence can't yet be used diagnostically.

Not only is there a multitude of communication difficulties, but there are also various kinds of definitions of language impairment. There are definitions in terms of deficits in the linguistic system; for example, 'phonological difficulties' where unintelligibility is caused by an immature or disordered sound system. There are definitions by exclusion; for example, specific language impairment which occurs in the absence of any cognitive or sensory impairments. There are also definitions based on comparing language skills with other cognitive skills, and those which focus on the functional implications of a deficit. Each type of definition is useful in different contexts; it is important to consider which is most helpful in identifying previously undetected communication problems and the communication difficulties which young people with emotional and behavioural difficulties often face.

Definitions of communication problems based on the linguistic description of language skills are of most use for research purposes. Children with communication difficulties experience problems with one or more of the components of the language system. So, for example, a child may have difficulty with the form of language such as following the rules for combining sounds into words, which could be called a 'phonological disability', or difficulty combining words into sentences appropriately, which is a 'grammatical disability'. Bishop (1992) defines 'pragmatic language disorder' as including problems understanding discourse (even though there is sufficient understanding at sentence level), lack of semantic specificity and a tendency to dominate a conversation with apparent disregard for the listener's needs. This kind of definition is useful in understanding the nature and heterogeneity of communication problems, but the limitation of this approach is that the practical implications of these problems are not always clear (Dockrell *et al.* 1997). For example, a child may have a grammatical disability and omit past tense endings, but knowing this gives no indication of the extent to which communication is impaired for that particular child.

Exclusionary criteria are used to define 'specific language impairments' by describing them as those which are not attributable to other factors. There seems to be a group of people who have great difficulty learning and using language, though they have no other recognisable cognitive impairment. (Whether this is actually the case or not is hotly debated.) In other words, specific language impairments are communication difficulties which occur in the absence of learning disability, neurological disability (for example, cerebral palsy), emotional problems or hearing loss (Tallal 1988). This type of definition is important in investigating 'pure' communication disorders but it is not very relevant here, since the aim is to consider communication problems which do co-exist with emotional and behavioural difficulties. However, the idea of excluding other possible causes of communication difficulty is a useful one as it can guide intervention. When assessing children with emotional and behavioural problems for communication difficulties, it is important to rule out possible confounding factors like attention deficits, which can appear to be comprehension difficulties. Children with Attention Deficit Hyperactivity Disorder (ADHD) have difficulty following instructions and listening and it is not always easy to determine whether this is due to comprehension difficulties or attention problems. However, if their inattention is more marked during verbal tasks it is reasonable to assume that a communication difficulty is a contributory factor. ADHD alone is more likely to be the cause if inattention is also present during tasks with fewer verbal demands (Prizant *et al.* 1990). It is also important not to assume that communication difficulties are due to the most obvious factors. If a young person is bilingual this does not preclude them from also having a specific language deficit.

Communication problems can also be defined in terms of discrepancy criteria (Aram, Morris and Hall 1993). Discrepancy criteria define language impairments in comparison to other non-impaired aspects of cognitive function, such as non-verbal intelligence. Discrepancy criteria are supposed to identify children who need intervention because their communication skills are significantly below expectations of children of that developmental level. Leonard (1998) suggests that, to be considered language-impaired, a child's verbal IQ should be at least 15 points below his or her non-verbal IQ. However, many young people with communication problems do not have this kind of verbal IQ deficit. There are also those with normally developing language who would meet these criteria for language impairment (Francis *et al.* 1996). Also, poverty may cause a child to score artificially low on IQ tests. Therefore, language impairments may be overlooked if discrepancy criteria are used (Lesser, Fifer and Clark 1965). Francis *et al.* (1996) also argue that the role of IQ tests in identifying communication difficulties is unwarranted, because IQ does not directly influence the acquisition of language skills. Another problem with using this type of criteria is that it is difficult to assess non-verbal skills; even tests of non-verbal intelligence require the use of language skills (Lahey 1990), so children with language deficits may fail on these tasks too, further invalidating the idea of a verbal/non-verbal discrepancy.

Discrepancies between chronological age and 'language' age are also used to detect communication impairment. However, there is debate about how wide the discrepancy between language age and chronological age has to be before a child is considered to be language impaired; it varies in the literature from six months to four years (Dunn *et al.* 1996). The significance of a two-year language delay will also vary depending on the age of the child or young person. Also, there is considerable variation in the rate at which all children acquire language (Bates, Dale and Thal 1995; Fenson *et al.* 1994), so it is not always clear where *abnormal* development is occurring. In addition, it seems to be the case that individuals not only vary in the rate at which they learn language, but also in their pattern of development (Bates and

McWhinney 1987). Therefore, atypical development clearly cannot solely be evaluated in comparison with developmental norms. Funding can also be relevant here; if perhaps there is only funding for the lowest 2 per cent of the population to receive help (as in some parts of the US), only this portion of the population will be defined as communication-impaired. Another difficulty with using developmental 'norms' is that most research into language development has been carried out on preschool and young school-aged children, so there are few norms available for adolescent language. There is also marked variability in the language abilities of adolescents who do not have communication problems, which adds to the difficulty in identifying deviations from the 'norm' (Menyuk 1977; Shapiro and Kalogerakis 1997). The way an adolescent communicates is also greatly influenced by the demands of the task as well as other factors (Scott 1988). Therefore, making comparisons with developmental norms is not always feasible or useful. Generally speaking, discrepancy formulae are problematic for the diagnosis of learning disabilities (Council for Learning Disabilities 1986).

Perhaps the most useful definition for identifying communication problems is in terms of the practical effects of these difficulties for the person experiencing them. Naremore, Densmore and Harman (1995) provide a definition of some communication problems thus: '...a school aged language impaired child is one who cannot use language to meet the demands of the social and/or academic contexts of the school' (p.3).

They also stress the fact that a child can be language impaired while 'wearing' another label, such as learning disabled. Of course, this also applies to children who are labelled as 'emotionally and behaviourally disordered'. This functional definition is the most useful, as, if there are children who are not able to learn or interact appropriately because of communication difficulties, it is important to identify them. Communication difficulties identified by any other means, without reference to their practical consequences, may not really exist as problems for the child or young person who experiences them. Indeed, the young person concerned, or their carers, may be the best judges of whether or not they are experiencing difficulties with communication, though they may not be able to explain or define them.

With remediation in mind, it is necessary to consider not only the question 'Is there a communication difficulty?' but also 'What is the specific nature of the deficit?' Having identified a difficulty, it is important to gather as much information about its nature as possible and this will also influence the choice of assessments used to identify communication problems. Some kinds of assessment may be useful for identification per se, but other forms of assessment may provide more useful descriptive information for developing teaching and therapy plans.

Which language skills should be assessed?

Before identifying an assessment tool it is necessary to decide which communication skills should be assessed. There is a large range of assessments to choose from, none of which assess all communication skills. So, decisions have to be made about where to start with an assessment and indeed when to stop. The choice of assessment will obviously be influenced by its aim. Ideally, one would choose to assess those language areas which are most likely to be indicative of a wider communication problem, or those where problems are most likely to occur. Although there is some research in this area (Bishop, North and Donlan 1996), we are still not sure which language deficits might be indicative of a wider communication difficulty, particularly in children who have emotional and behavioural difficulties. However, there are some indications about which areas are more likely to be impaired.

Some, including Campbell *et al.* (1997), would argue that sound processing problems (in the absence of a hearing loss) are at the root of many communication difficulties. Interestingly, Giddan *et al.* (1996) found a high proportion of children with previously unsuspected communication problems (and emotional and behavioural problems) had such sound processing difficulties. Therefore, assessments that attempt to measure a child's linguistic processing capabilities rather than their ability to use language might help to identify the fundamental language processing difficulties, which are the basis of communication problems in some children.

Pragmatics, which encompasses the 'use' of language socially, has been identified as a particular area of difficulty in children with emotional and behavioural problems (Baltaxe and Simmons 1988a, 1988b; McDonough 1989). Social communication difficulties contribute significantly to the difficulties young people with emotional and behavioural difficulties have with interacting. These young people have difficulty with skills such as giving an appropriate amount of information, appreciating another person's point of view and being aware of how the context influences communication. Therefore, an assessment of social communication skills, or the way they use language, is an important part of any assessment of a young person with emotional and behavioural difficulties.

It has also been shown that comprehension difficulties are prevalent in children who have emotional and behavioural difficulty. Part of this is due to difficulty in understanding specific abstract concepts such as time, space and emotion vocabulary (Giddan 1991). Such difficulties are common amongst many children with communication difficulties. Young people with comprehension difficulty also tend to have problems understanding complex sentences, such as 'the horse she fell off was a white one', and non-literal language, such as 'get a grip'. Making inferences from verbal clues can also be very difficult for them.

Language-impaired students often have difficulty acquiring the rules for complex sentences (Wiig and Secord 1992) (for example, the water reaches boiling point *because* of the increase in energy) and this also applies to young people with emotional and behavioural problems. Many young people with communication difficulties also have particular problems with getting tenses right (Rice *et al.* 1998). In addition to this, language-impaired young people often find it difficult to construct meaningful narratives, as this requires adequate functioning in basic language domains such as grammar and vocabulary, as well as the ability to summarise and sequence events. Therefore, narrative skills will not develop if there are difficulties in these areas (Snow 1998). Narrative skills are often particularly problematic for young people with emotional and behavioural difficulties. To be able to tell a story, one needs not only mastery of the structure of language, its grammar and vocabulary, but also to be able to coherently sequence events, to be able to take the viewpoint of the characters and to appreciate the listener's knowledge and perspective. The way language-impaired children recall narratives seems to be qualitatively different from that of other children, in that they tend not to link the events in the story and they may also omit key information (Swartzlander and Naremore 1989). Children with language impairment also tend to give less information about the characters and to leave out information about the internal responses of the characters, such as their mental state or emotional responses (Gillam and Carlile 1997).

Narrative problems are predictors of overall prognosis; young people who have this kind of difficulty are likely to have persistent communication difficulties (Botting *et al.* 2001). Adolescent language-impaired students often have problems with self-monitoring and with the organisational structure of a story, providing enough detail and elaboration and maintaining logical consistency throughout the narrative (Wiig 1995). Young people with psychiatric illness also have difficulties with narratives, but their problems tend to be more with its flow than its structure. They use more fillers ('um', 'er' etc.), repetitions and repairs than other children (Vallance, Im and Cohen 1999). Children with schizophrenia find narrative discourse particularly difficult, appearing to have illogical thinking, loose association between events and poverty of speech content (Caplan 1996). Therefore, a careful analysis of the narrative structure of children with emotional and behavioural difficulties could prove useful in identifying communication problems, and differentiating them from other difficulties. However, there may well be some overlap between what is considered to be a linguistic problem and what is seen as a thought disorder, as the 'loose associations' which are part of a thought disorder are very similar to the way that children with pragmatic difficulties give insufficient or ambiguous information in narratives which are not logically linked.

Wiig and Secord (1992) found that 60 to 75 per cent of children with language disabilities have content deficits; that is, difficulty expressing meaning. This is also true of children with emotional and behavioural difficulties who often have a limited vocabulary particularly as regards abstract concepts like emotions.

In adolescents, language impairments change in nature, so additional types of assessment may be necessary. Adolescents with communication difficulties are often unable to integrate linguistic and social rules, shared knowledge and emotional needs. This is because language is a powerful tool for organising and sequencing events, which they lack. Language skills are also important for recognising patterns, thus providing 'scripts' for certain common events such as completing an assignment or test. These kinds of reasoning skills are unfortunately often absent in children with language disabilities, so they also have to be considered in any assessment (Meltzer 1992).

It must be stressed that any area of language could be impaired so, although we have some clues as to what to assess, it is important to get as full a picture as possible.

A holistic approach

The holistic approach to assessment stresses the inter-relatedness of language, cognition and affect, and it is increasingly used in the identification and treatment of communication difficulties (Gerber 1993). The holistic approach considers the young person's communicative strengths and weaknesses and the effects of the latter, as well as the context in which these occur. It also tries to understand the young person's overall development, their family and community situation and their sense of self and social effectiveness.

The holistic approach assumes that an assessment of communication skills is part of an assessment of the young person's overall functioning, but of course this is not always the case. Nonetheless, it is important to gather information about other areas of functioning apart from communication. Developmental and other background information is crucial, particularly if the young person appears to have complex needs (though such information is often lacking in children in the care of the local authority). Information about cognitive skills, and other non-verbal skills, can also be useful. An assessor must also be aware of the typical stages of child development, for example in levels of attention. During testing, observations can be made about attention levels and response times, both of which will affect the young person's functioning in class and socially. Hearing status is particularly significant in this context, as hearing impairment will affect communication in specific ways. If a young person is unintelligible it may be necessary to examine the structure and function of the lips, tongue and soft palate.

No single assessment can evaluate the complex interplays between language cognition and emotion, so a holistic approach will usually include a mixture of formal and informal assessments as well as observation and interviewing 'significant others'. Another feature of the holistic approach is that assessment is on-going rather than a one-off event.

An important part of the assessment process is gathering information from people who know the child or young person well. Parents or carers are often the best sources of information about young children; teachers, tutors or therapists can also provide useful information about how older children communicate. It is important for the interviewer to collaborate with these 'significant others' and to enable them to take an active part in the assessment process. If there is good collaboration during the assessment process then this can be therapeutic in itself, because a greater understanding of the communication difficulties a young person faces enables significant adults to modify their interaction to facilitate communication.

As regards communication skills, a holistic approach means that it is important to consider the form, content and use of a young person's communications, since language deficits can impact on all of these areas. This means there should be an assessment of the way a young person constructs words and sentences, the meanings they convey and the way they use language socially (see Chapter 2 for more details). Law and Conway (1989) suggest that a thorough assessment of communication skills is particularly important in children with emotional and behavioural difficulties, as focusing on one area and neglecting any other can result in a misleading picture. The precise nature of the assessment will depend on the child's age and abilities. For preverbal children, their 'use' of language will be mainly vocalisations and gestures and may also include signs or symbols. It is important to determine which communicative functions are being expressed. Sometimes children will use unusual or unacceptable ways of communicating, and these should be recognised and analysed as a first step towards helping the development of more acceptable forms of communication (Wetherby and Prizant 1992).

A holistic approach would also include using a mixture of formal testing, informal assessment and observations, in order to gather a variety of useful information. A 'triangulation' of data gathered in different ways will help to build up an accurate picture of any communication difficulties. For example, comprehension can be assessed in context and it can be assessed in a decontextualised situation by formal testing. If both methods indicate difficulties, it is more likely that they are significant for the young person. Expressive language assessment also needs to occur in different ways; the nature of the task, as well as many other factors, will influence the complexity of the language the young person uses, so the use of a variety of assessments will lead to a truer picture.

Assessing the communication skills of young people with emotional and behavioural difficulties

A young person who has emotional and behavioural difficulties has them for a reason; knowledge of their family background and developmental, emotional and medical history are crucial to understanding them. Unfortunately, if a young person is in public care, good sources of information may be lost because they are living away from home. If they have only recently moved into public care, or into a new placement, then it is possible that no one knows them well. Records are often incomplete, so this further adds to the difficulty, and to the time it will take to get a clear and accurate history. However, as well as knowing as much as is possible about a young person, an open mind is also necessary. Often young people with emotional and behavioural problems have a considerable negative reputation, which is often worth ignoring. It is important to have positive expectations of them because what you expect of someone can be a self-fulfilling prophecy. Low self-esteem often means that young people with emotional and behavioural difficulties don't expect much of themselves, so meeting someone with positive expectations of them can make a big difference. Day-to-day information is also important during an assessment, as events in the young person's life, such as a parent leaving home, a pending court case, a change of placement or their teacher being on a course, can markedly affect how they respond.

Consent for an assessment has to be gained from whoever has parental responsibility, and of course the young person himself or herself. Confidentiality is also an issue here, and it is important to be clear about who the assessment is for and who will have access to it. The young person involved needs a clear explanation of the purpose of the assessment, including the possible outcomes and their implications. Clearly, all of this has to be carefully and sensitively done, but honesty is important, as it is an integral part of the process of gaining trust and co-operation. Co-operation can be encouraged, depending on the child's age, either through intrinsic rewards, such as 'this will help me help you to understand what your teacher says', or extrinsic rewards, such as 'let's do this, then you can choose something to play with for five minutes'.

The environment in which the assessment takes place will have an impact on the results. A clinical setting is anxiety-provoking for most people; therefore, it is important that assessments are carried out in a variety of situations. Young children will be more relaxed, but possibly more distracted, at home. A school-aged child might find it easier to complete formal assessment if they have already met the tester, perhaps when they came to observe them in class. Ideally, a room for formal testing should not be intimidating, but a quiet, comfortable place free of distractions. If there are lots of things on the walls, you may need to allow time for the young person to explore and look at them.

Being assessed is emotionally charged. It is best to acknowledge this and to be very sensitive to how the young person is feeling. They need time to get to know and trust the assessor. They should be encouraged to say how they feel, and to say when they're tired or when they need to let off steam. Planning and flexibility are both important; the assessor must be willing to negotiate about the order of events, and how much 'work' the young person does. Young people with emotional and behavioural difficulties may be anxious, eager to please, uncooperative or passive. (There is never a dull moment.) They may also have short attention spans and be distractible, so it is wise to have a variety of activities available so that ones which are motivating, and at the right level of difficulty, can be used. It is necessary to be responsive to the young person because it is often impossible to predict how they'll be feeling and what they'll be happy to do. Children with emotional and behavioural difficulties can become non-compliant or oppositional when the demands of the task are beyond them, or when they do not understand what to do. If this happens, it is important to have a change of activity available and acknowledge 'I didn't explain that very well' or 'That doesn't make any sense, does it? Let's do something else.' If a young person has a short attention span, frequent changes of activity and 'rest periods' will help them focus for longer.

Flexibility and listening to the young person is also vital because you can't predict what will be enjoyable or reinforcing for them, or what they'll hate. But they will find a way of communicating this. For some children, an unstructured 'free play' situation is extremely anxiety-producing, while others find it relaxing. Some respond well to being given clear choices, though others will find this stressful. Many children prefer structure and a clear list of 'jobs' to be done during the session, but others will find this daunting. It may be necessary to modify tests, often because they can't all be completed in one attempt, but careful note should be taken of how and why it is done, as this provides useful information, and it may also affect the way the results are interpreted. Uncooperativeness is often cited as a reason why a young person could not be assessed; however, what can't be assessed is as important as what can, so these are all useful clues. Information gathered from others and observations are particularly important if a young person is not keen to undertake formal assessment.

A holistic approach is extremely important with young people who have emotional and behavioural difficulties. Involving the family where possible, and other people who know the child well, will help determine whether their behaviour and responses in the assessment process are typical. If the results from different assessments concur they are easier to interpret, although of course the opposite is also true! It is likely that assessing the communication skills of a young person with emotional and behavioural difficulties will be very time-consuming.

Standardised assessment

Researchers and clinicians often identify communication difficulties by using standardised tests, which attempt to compare a child's performance with a cross-section of the population in order to identify untypical behaviour (Stark and Tallal 1981). Standardised tests aim to provide quantifiable, objective and repeatable measures of language skills.

Standardised, norm-referenced tests are designed and developed in a detailed and lengthy process in an attempt to make them as valid and reliable as possible. This means they should assess what they aim to in a consistent way. A useful standardised test should be both sensitive and specific. Its sensitivity is the accuracy with which it identifies language impairment and its specificity is the degree to which it identifies normally developing language (Merrell and Plante 1997). Extension testing can add to the validity of a score because it is a way of checking whether a young person 'really' has difficulties in a certain area which has been identified by the assessment. This is often useful before learning objectives are set. In order to maintain validity, standardised tests must be used precisely as their authors suggest. The use of individual subtests, rather than the whole assessment, can invalidate the results, and is therefore not accurate enough for diagnostic decisions. (However, in practice, few children with emotional and behavioural problems can cope with a whole standardised assessment at once.) The main value of standardised assessments is the comparison they allow with other young people of the same age. Standardised scores, which compare a young person's performance to those of a sample of their peers, are more useful than age equivalent scores (Wiig 1995). In other words, just because an eight-year-old gains an age equivalent of five years on a test does not mean that his or her performance is outside the normal range; only a standard score can give that information. The choice of test will depend on the age and developmental level of the child or young person and the purpose of the assessment.

Despite standardisation, formal assessments vary in how they define language impairment. Different tests employ different criteria for determining where a communication problem occurs; some will use one standard deviation below the norm, some three standard deviations (Merrell and Plante 1997), so this must be borne in mind when comparing test results. Different researchers may also use different criteria. Cohen and Lipsett (1991), in their study of children with unsuspected communication problems, defined language problems as occurring when a child gained scores which were one standard deviation below the mean on two out of seven standardised tests. Others, such as Giddan *et al.* (1996), combined standard scores with 'clinical judgement' to determine whether a communication problem was present.

One of the major problems with formal assessment is that most language tests were standardised using only children who had normally developing language. This means that whatever score criteria are used on a standardised test for 'language impaired', there will be some children with normally developing language who gain that score. For example, in the standardisation of the CELF (Clinical Evaluation of Language Fundamentals), children who were having speech and language therapy were excluded, yet it aims to identify children who are in need of such help.

Formal standardised assessments also have other flaws. They are not always sensitive or specific. These kinds of assessments have been shown to overidentify children with normally developing language (Aram *et al.* 1991), and to underidentify children with specific language impairment (Aram *et al.* 1993). One reason for this inaccuracy is the standardisation population; any test becomes less useful as the population it is used with differs from this original population. The young people being tested should be comparable to the population on which it was standardised (Russell and Sternberg 1997), but this is rarely the case. Until recently, many assessments were only standardised on American children or on small samples. Therefore the results gained from such tests were only applicable to British children with caution. Merrell and Plante (1997) researched the usefulness of some formal tests by using them on a local sample of children already identified as communication-impaired or with normally developing language. They recommend the development of such local databases to improve the accuracy of formal assessments, since it would help determine an appropriate cut-off point for where a disability exists. This begs the questions, how were those already identified actually identified? Is a test valid if it agrees with other tests? Burgess and Bransby (1990) used all the formal assessments that they were employing to identify communication problems in children with emotional and behavioural problems, on a population of ordinary children. The validity of these tests was confirmed, as the typically developing children scored well above expected levels.

There are also problems in comparing across tests, as they probably have different normative samples. This means that comparisons of different areas of language function must only be made with caution, as must considerations of verbal versus non-verbal functioning. Similarly, total scores can be misleading if there is a wide variation in individual subtest scores. Often, the way a young person completes the task is as interesting as their score. Error patterns and the strategies they use provide useful information. It is also important to take into account the other skills which are necessary to take part in a formal language assessment; attention, motivation, visual and auditory skills and memory may all be necessary and if they are lacking they will affect the results.

Further criticisms of formal assessments are that they are biased against children from minority backgrounds, because they rely on experiential history as well as vocabulary knowledge (Campbell *et al.* 1997). Over- and under-diagnosis of communication difficulties is more likely to occur in children who are not white and middle class, as they tend to be underrepresented in the populations used to standardise normative tests, as are young people whose first language is not English.

Using formal assessments of language skills as the only measure of communication skills will not identify all communication difficulties. These tests only measure certain aspects of language, for example vocabulary or grammar. There are very few tests which measure a child's ability to understand discourse, converse, or to construct a narrative, which are the sorts of task to be faced in school.

Another, often more significant, problem with formal assessment is its artificiality. Formal testing is by its very nature an unusual situation, which does not necessarily call for functional language. This is especially true where an assessor has to give instructions in a precise way, and is not allowed to give the young person any feedback, only general encouragement. The assessment situation itself can also be unfamiliar and intimidating and this could also skew the results. Fulk, Brugham and Lohman (1998) reported that children with emotional and behavioural problems experienced more test anxiety than other groups of students, and that their co-operation might also be more difficult to gain. Some authors have minimised the amount of formal assessment used, in order to reduce children's anxieties. Blager (1979) felt that children who had been abused or neglected were often fearful or resistant to testing, so she only used those tests which required a non-verbal response.

Formal assessments compare a child's performance with developmental norms rather than seeking out factors typical of abnormal development, so this may also make them less useful in identifying communication difficulties. Merrell and Plante (1997) found that although some tests were accurate in identifying communication problems, they were not that good at identifying specific deficits, and other types of assessment could be a more effective way of gathering this information. Formal assessments can be useful in tracking development and in assessing the effectiveness of speech and language therapy but they may not be fine grained enough to identify all developments.

Informal assessments

Informal assessments occur in less formal situations and are not standardised but they can still be detailed and systematic. Their major advantage is their flexibility. The most obvious disadvantage of informal assessments is that it is not necessarily possible to compare results to 'norms'. Such assessments may be much more use with low functioning individuals or where it is difficult to gain co-operation. There are also situations where it is not possible to use standardised assessment because modifications have to be made, perhaps because the young person needs to use some form of communication aid. In some areas of communication, formal assessments may not exist or norms may not be available. For example, children with semantic-pragmatic difficulties might be verbose or answer questions too literally (Bishop 1998) and this would not be identified by any formal assessment. Such skills are also difficult to assess formally, as norms are problematic to define because the rules of social interaction vary depending on the time, place, culture and the individuals involved.

It is generally recommended that, as well as formal assessment, additional information should be gathered to determine whether a child really has a communication difficulty or not (Tomblin 1983). I would argue that this is vital. Some authors suggest that the most useful information about children with emotional and behavioural difficulties will be found in dynamic-interactive assessment, functional assessment and observational methods (Rock *et al.* 1997). This section will consider the merits of these and other kinds of informal assessments.

Observation

Direct observation of the way a young person uses language in 'real' situations is often one of the most informative types of assessment. Bashir *et al.* (1983) argue that standardised tests can say something about a child's strengths and weaknesses, but only observations can tell us if the child can cope with the language demands of the environment. Samples of expressive language show that children who have communication difficulties make more errors in spontaneous speech than other children (Dunn *et al.* 1996). Informal observational assessments have the advantage of being representative of how the child or young person communicates, though they must be undertaken in a systematic way (and bearing in mind that being observed may alter the way a child interacts). It is important that observations occur in settings which are important for the child's development (Barnett, Carey and Hall 1993). One major advantage of observation is that it might highlight strengths or weaknesses that hadn't been noticed before.

It seems deceptively simple, but in practice observation can be very time-consuming, and difficult to interpret. It is hard to know whether what you have seen is representative, or significant, and to what extent the presence of an observer has affected the outcome. However, an awareness of these factors and the development of an alliance between the observer, observed and those who know the young person well can minimise them. There is also the issue of recording the observations to consider. In order not to forget anything, important recording has to be done at the time, or soon after. Video-taping is especially useful, as it allows for assessment of non-verbal as well as verbal cues, and it is objective. But it can also be more intrusive than, for example, a small mini-disc recorder. The issue of consent is very relevant here; often young people are not keen to be videoed or tape-recorded, and this has to be respected. There are various checklists of communicative behaviours which will help identify areas of strength and weakness, and which can be completed after a period of observation. These have the advantage of being unobtrusive, though they will focus, and thereby limit, the observations recorded. The Children's Communicative Checklist (Bishop 1998) was designed to assess aspects of the use of language (amongst others) and it is a useful tool because it requires someone with knowledge of the young person, gained through observation over at least three months, to complete it, and then the results can be compared with a standardisation sample.

An observation of a child's interactions with caregivers provides valuable information; it allows communicative styles to be identified, some of which may be more useful as regards enabling language development than others. Important areas to be considered are whether the child's attempts at communication are accepted or rejected, whether the adult directs the interaction, or whether there is responsiveness to the child. Clearly, this kind of observation can be very stressful for the adults involved and therefore it should be sensitively handled. Interpreting what is seen is not straightforward either, and there is no guarantee that what is observed is really representative of ongoing interactions. Carer–child interactions should also be considered in the wider context, as cultural differences will impact on what is observed, as well as its interpretation.

For young children, an observation of play is useful. Not only will it provide information on verbal and non-verbal communication and interaction, but it also gives clues to other areas of a child's development, such as cognitive and emotional development. For example, symbolic pretend play can give indications about how a child's theory of mind is developing. Teddy won't get fed unless the child understands that others may also feel hunger. An empty spoon will only be used to feed teddy if a child has enough symbolic appreciation to realise that an empty spoon can represent a real one with food on it. As language (which is another symbolic activity) develops, children are gradually able to 'set the scene' in play, with words rather than real props. Language is also used to develop themes or scripts for play (for example, going to the doctor, or army games), and to negotiate roles within these themes. The play situation observed may or may not be structured depending on the child and the aim of the assessment, but obviously this will affect the information gathered.

Observing older children in school, in lessons and at play, can be very informative as there is a great deal to be learnt about how to act and communicate in these situations. Observations in school will provide information about how well the student copes with the demands of the curriculum, and if, and how, their communication difficulties impair learning. However, trying to observe a young person in school can affect everyone else in the room. Other students may be curious, and adults can feel threatened; therefore it is important to explain one's aims and expectations of this kind of exercise, and to feed back findings promptly.

Interviews

Interviews are a useful way to gain information, from the young person themselves as well as from others who know them well. However, young people with communication difficulties may find this kind of investigation particularly difficult, because it involves skills they are not proficient in. Useful information about a young person can be gained through interviewing their significant others as regards behaviours, learning styles and relationships.

The way questions are phrased directly affects the answers received. Descriptive information is far more informative than judgements or explanations, so questions should be carefully worded. Also, an open question such as 'Tell me about a typical day in your life' will get a very different answer to 'Do you have problems talking to people?' Obviously, the young person's expressive language skills will also affect the answer. If they have communication difficulty they may be able to respond to a question which requires a 'yes' or 'no' answer, but not be able to formulate a response to an open question.

Interviews may have set questions planned in advance, or they may follow the informant's train of thought. In an unstructured interview, where specific questions are not determined in advance, it is possible to seek examples, descriptions and explanations; this may not be possible in a structured interview, where answering a series of questions can interrupt the respondent's train of thought and make them feel less able to elaborate. A semi-structured interview format is probably most useful, as it has enough structure to ensure that no important questions are forgotten, but also flexibility which allows for responsiveness to the interviewee and for negotiation of meaning to take place, so that both parties can be sure that they understand each other. It is enlightening in itself to use an interview that allows the respondent to answer in his or her own terms.

The process of being interviewed can be therapeutic in itself, because someone is willing to listen and trying to understand any difficulties faced. This can also be a disadvantage because of the time necessary to do it thoroughly. Much depends on the characteristics of the interviewer and whether they are able to make the interviewee comfortable enough to be forthcoming and keep them on track. Interviews can, of course, also be intimidating if not carried out sensitively.

Criterion referenced testing

One of the disadvantages of observational assessment is that a young person need not do what they find difficult. It is often necessary to 'stress' their language skills in order to identify areas of weakness (Lahey 1990). When they are observed in a naturalistic setting, young people may seem to be able to converse with their peers adequately. However, it may not be until the same young people are observed in class, where the style and vocabulary of the interaction are very different, that it becomes clear that they have communication difficulties. Another example of this is children with comprehension problems, who talk all the time because then they don't have to try and understand what someone else is saying. It would be difficult to identify their communication problems by just observing such individuals.

Criterion referenced probes are an informal assessment which can be used to see how pupils perform in response to specific situational demands. An example of this is whether they know and can use the vocabulary required for a history project, for example words ending in '-ism' ('colonialism', 'racism' etc.). It is also possible to assess how much of a lesson pupils understood and retained by observing the lesson, then talking to them about it afterwards (Nelson 1989). These types of assessments can be used to identify features of communication difficulties which are often noted in clinical accounts, but which are not assessed by formal assessments (Bishop 1998). Criterion referenced tests are useful once communication difficulties have been identified, but would not necessarily discriminate from other learning difficulties or help to identify communication problems. These are also useful where norm referenced tests are not available, where the standardisation is not appropriate or where information about very specific language skills is needed (McCauley 1996).

Self-assessment

The young people themselves may have views about whether they have a communication problem and, if so, its nature. Their views are particularly important with remediation in mind, as the students need to take ownership of any communication difficulties in order to address them. Self-assessments can take the form of an audiotape recording, a written account or flow diagram, or perhaps an interview procedure with open questions (Wiig 1995); for example, how do you deal with problems understanding classroom instructions?

Dynamic assessment

Dynamic assessment is an assessment of learning rather than skills, and it is a useful adjunct to formal assessment, because it gives some indication of the young person's potential. Sometimes young people have communication deficits because they have not had opportunities to learn the relevant skills, rather than because they are unable to learn these skills, and dynamic assessment can help to differentiate these two groups of young people. Dynamic assessment considers what young people can do, with and without support, and how they learn. It is possible to use dynamic assessment to assess a child's narrative abilities (Gillam, Pena and Miller 1999). This involves teaching a narrative skill that the child has not yet acquired, for example how to use settings, and observing how well the child is able to learn and use this information. Children who are not language-impaired can easily improve their narratives with such individual support, but language-impaired children need much more focused individual help. Not all cultures emphasise sequencing, so it is important to consider this in relation to young people from non-dominant cultures, but if they are able to learn some sequencing from a brief period of input it is unlikely that they have a significant problem in this area.

Linguistic processing

Another kind of assessment which taps into underlying skills, perhaps those particularly impaired in young people with communication difficulties, is an assessment of linguistic processing abilities. Auditory information processing is critical for language development and impairment. Tests of linguistic processing abilities are useful because they are not reliant on previous knowledge, language or context, but they provide information about how language is processed. An example of this kind of assessment is asking a child to repeat a non-word, for example 'tep'; only those with an intact sound processing capacity will find this sort of task easy.

There is evidence that children with communication difficulties repeat non-words less accurately than their peers with normally developing language, and (obviously) that this discrepancy is not due to a lack of word knowledge (Montgomery 1995). Nathan, Stackhouse and Goulandris (1998) have also found that non-word repetition, amongst other speech processing difficulties, is poorer in children with speech and language impairment and that it may also be relevant to the subsequent development of literacy problems. Difficulties in repeating non-words may even be characteristic of some kinds of inherited communication problems (Bishop *et al.* 1996). Dollaghan and Campbell (1998) found that this measure of language difficulties might be better than formal assessments at identifying language-impaired children. This could be relevant to communication problems in children with emotional and behavioural difficulties since Giddan *et al.* (1996) found a high proportion of children, who had previously unrecognised language and speech problems, had sound-processing deficits. However, Bailey and Snowling (2002) point out that not all children with language defects have auditory processing problems.

Identification of communication difficulties by non-speech and language therapists

There is a rich source of information about a young person's communication skills in the observations of everyone who talks with them. This kind of information can also validate other assessments. Conti-Ramsden, Crutchley and Botting (1997) found that test results supplemented with teachers' opinions led to a coherent pattern of results about a student's communication difficulties and no doubt the same is true when carers' opinions are included.

However, large scale screening tests for early language delay may not be effective. Some (Law *et al.* 1998) suggest that health visitors asking parents if their child has a problem is as effective as using a screening test. However, Pickstone (2003) found that workers without a professional training were able to carry out an effective screening for children with language delay as part of a *Sure Start* (Glass 2001) initiative.

Other professionals may be reluctant to try to identify communication problems. Secord and Wiig (1992) have found that teachers were often reluctant to complete formal checklists about a child's communication skills. This was partly because of the use of technical language in the checklists and partly because they felt this was the speech and language pathologist's job. Secord and Wiig (1992) solved this problem by asking teachers to make incidental notes whenever a given student experienced a communication failure, and this seemed more effective. Burgess and Bransby (1990) reported that the teachers in their study were given guidelines for identifying language disabled children, but these did not actually help them identify children with communication difficulties. Their conclusion was that teachers need training in identifying speech and language problems as well as written guidelines, rather than guidelines alone.

There are various 'indicators' of communication difficulty which can help non-specialists decide whether a referral for a fuller assessment is necessary (see Afasic 2003 and Appendix 1), but in my experience these are not useful unless the person using them knows the young person well and unless they have also had some training about communication difficulties beforehand.

Conclusion

There are various informal and formal methods of assessing language skills, all of which have advantages and disadvantages. No individual method is likely to provide a satisfactory assessment of a child's communication skills, and indeed relying on formal assessment could be misleading. The most useful assessment of communication skills is likely to be one which uses a variety of strategies, including formal and informal methods, and which assesses a variety of language functions in various situations.

CHAPTER 6

What Can be Done to Help Young People with Communication and Emotional and Behavioural Problems?

Introduction

For every complex problem there is always a simple answer, and it is usually wrong. Young people with complex difficulties, including emotional behavioural and communication difficulties, need carefully thought-out help in order to overcome them. Simple measures, though often helpful, are unlikely to be enough. Nonetheless, there are some straightforward interventions that everyone working with a young person with complex difficulties can undertake which can make a difference. Both simple and more 'complex' types of interventions will be discussed in this chapter. The first part of an effective set of strategies is good assessment, which is vital to determine the young person's particular strengths and weaknesses. This is necessary for planning, but also to ensure that they are not over- or underestimated. For a successful answer to a complex problem, professionals from different disciplines need to share their insights with each other, and with the young people and their family or carers, working together to form and carry out a plan of action.

In considering possible solutions to complex emotional, behavioural and communication difficulties it is important to consider:

- factors within the child or young person
- factors in the environment
- factors in interactions with the child.

Although there is much yet to be learnt about what the most useful interventions might be, intervention is necessary because young people with emotional, behavioural and communication difficulties are unlikely to just grow out of them. However, there is considerable plasticity in the developing brain, so the potential for change, given the right environment, is significant. The brain also continues to have the potential for development into adulthood and this must not be overlooked. It must be stressed that what follows is by no means an exhaustive list of possible interventions, neither can any specific intervention be described in detail here, but simply an overview of the types of intervention which can be useful.

Broad strategies

Prevention and early intervention

There is significant evidence about the long-lasting and far-reaching effects of impaired early interactions, particularly in an abusive or neglectful relationship. Such interaction difficulties can lead to, and perpetuate, communication and emotional and cognitive difficulties in the child. Therefore, early intervention to encourage parents to be responsive to their child's attempts at communication can lead to improvements in behaviour and communication (Hancock, Kaiser and Delaney 2002). Indeed, it is generally thought that any interventions (whether it is the communication or the behavioural difficulty that appears to be 'primary') are more successful if begun early. There is a considerable body of research which enables us to identify those children who are at risk of emotional, behavioural, learning and communication difficulties, so monitoring their progress to enable early intervention where necessary is crucial. Given their intertwining nature, any early intervention for behavioural difficulties should also consider the possibility of language deficits.

Although early intervention is important, early diagnosis can be very difficult. Some children may be diagnosed as having pervasive developmental disorder (which is on the autistic continuum), because they have impaired social interaction, communication, language development, and stereotypical behaviours. However, Mukaddes et al. (2000) found a population of such children in whom these deficits were associated with what they called 'pathological care', and a treatment programme aimed at improving interactions produced an improvement in early interactive behaviours and language development.

Early identification of communication difficulties and intervention is important because of the role that communication skills play in the development of emotional, social and cognitive skills. Communication intervention may pre-empt behaviour problems in children. Preventing communication difficulties from developing or persisting could also reduce the possibility of some of the negative consequences of communication difficulties, such as educational failure and psychiatric difficulties.

In intervening early, the family is the most appropriate context, ideally with the family members being the most involved. Developing communication skills through everyday routines is most effective for young children, so the family needs to be involved in setting these kinds of goals. One way of helping young people develop interaction skills and resilience is through supporting their families where necessary, as well as helping them to develop external support systems. In this way, families may be able to provide emotional support as well as support for learning. Social work services, including intensive 'Family Preservation Services', aim to strengthen families, empowering them and enabling them to access services, thereby improving outcomes for children. Family members may also need help with strategies to facilitate the child's development and to recognise their child's strengths and weaknesses. An outsider's perception of their child may be different from their own. It is important that these strategies and insights are offered in such a way as to be acceptable to the culture of the family. If a professional directly intervenes and interacts with a child they may 'unintentionally disempower a caregiver' (McDonough 1993). Parent management training, where parents are shown how to change the way they relate to their children, essentially by being consistent and rewarding positive behaviours, has been shown to be effective as a 'treatment' for conduct disorders (Brestan and Eyeberg 1998), particularly before adolescence. However, before any child or young person can make progress, his or her needs for basic physical care and safety must be met; if this is not the case, nothing else will develop.

Speech and language therapists often work with families to help early communication skills develop. Anderson-Wood and Smith (1997) suggest ways to develop the pragmatic skills (broadly the use of language) in children. They stress the importance of involving caregivers, and a conversational approach where client and therapist or carer has an equal share in the interaction. In order to do this, it is necessary to choose motivating activities which require communication with others. Speech and language therapists can support carers in their interactions with their children, but also suggest and demonstrate alternatives. They also have a role in helping them understand the communication skills of their child and the strategies currently in play. Speech and language therapists can also provide information about the next stages of development and, if appropriate, they can offer more successful strategies and help with their implementation in daily routines. Problem-solving workshops for parents/carers of children with communication diffi-culties have proved popular and valuable (Peck 2002).

As early interactions are so crucial, education and training about them for all parents is important. Support for new parents is also vital, particularly those in adverse situations. There are various initiatives which aim to support and educate families, and thereby prevent breakdowns in early interactions. *Home-Start* is a UK programme which aims to promote the welfare of families with at least one child under five, through offering families support, friendship and practical help (www.home-star.org.uk). The *Headstart* (2002) programme in the United States has shown that interventions which influence early interactions, particularly if they teach alternatives to harsh discipline have the potential to improve the quality of early interactions and language development. Similarly, *Sure Start* (2002) in the UK aims to improve the health and well-being of families and children in disadvantaged communities. It attempts to provide co-ordinated, flexible preventative services, and targets children under four with the aim that they should be 'ready to thrive' when they start school. It will also support families from early pregnancy till children are age 14, where necessary. Encouraging language development is an important part of these programmes. Other initiatives stress the importance of early communication skills. The National Literacy Trust is running a campaign called 'Talk to Your Baby, Developing Language for Life', in recog-nition of the fact that parents and carers have an important part to play in helping their children learn to use language (through listening and playing as well as by talking to them), and that language is the key to learning, particu-larly as regards literacy. The Hanen Early Language Parent Programme (Manolson 1992) enables groups of parents to learn about communication difficulties and strategies they can use to help language development. A Home Office initiative called On Track aims to prevent youth offending by inter-vening early. Speech and language therapists have become involved in this project because helping to develop communication skills could reduce offending behaviour; prisons are full of people with communication and literacy difficulties who might not be there if they had these skills. Most of these initiatives are new, although early indications are that they can be effective and they seem to offer hope for future generations.

A positive relationship

In order to help young people learn, they need to be in a safe and positive relationship with the person who wants to help them. Young people are more likely to achieve a positive outcome if they have the benefit of a good relationship with peers and adults, and this is particularly important for those who have been maltreated. They may take time to build up trust, but adults who are positive about them, and who have faith in their ability to learn and to change, can make a difference. There is a need to restore a sense of safety, control, consistency and predictability for any young person who has been in an adverse environment. Through this kind of relationship emotional and communication skills can develop.

Whatever the young person's background, any relationship with a worker should be based on genuine interest, respect and understanding as well as a celebration of differences, including cultural differences. Empathy and active listening are the foundation of this as it is important to listen carefully to young people and to be willing to try to see things from their point of view. Reliability is also paramount. Butler and Williamson (1994) found that young people in the care of the local authority want professionals to listen, be available, be non-judgemental and non-directive. They also valued adults with a sense of humour, who were honest and trustworthy. While humour is important, sarcasm can be very detrimental to a positive relationship, not least because young people with communication difficulties may take it literally and be puzzled and offended. A clear distinction needs to be made between responses to young people and to the way they behave; it is possible to be non-judgemental of young people, but not necessarily of their behaviour. A sense of belief in the young person can become a self-fulfilling prophecy. Consistent and appropriate expectations of the young person create a sense of security. Similarly, predictable routines and structure can help a young person feel safe and begin to relax. Confidentiality within the worker–young person interaction also helps to build trust. The young person needs to know what confidentiality means, how far it extends and when it might be broken (usually only if a child protection issue arises). If confidentiality has to be broken then the young person has to be informed and told why.

In order to develop communication skills, young people must have a need to communicate; being given choices and being allowed to make decisions empowers them to do this. Even very simple joint activity routines (Snyder-Mclean *et al.* 1984), such as peek-a-boo, allow children to take some control of the interaction, as they decide if they want more or not. As children grow, it is important to foster communication of needs and negotiation of differences; they will be more inclined to try and communicate if they know what they say will be heard and responded to. Although responsiveness is important, complete permissiveness could be dangerous, so there has to be a mixture of firm, fair boundaries as well as a willingness to respond to the young person's communications. Negative and controlling interactions do not benefit young people in any way and can be seriously detrimental to their learning and growth.

Adults working with young people who have communication and emotional and behavioural difficulties have to consider their own emotional awareness, because emotions are contagious. They must be able to tolerate the strong and distressing emotions that the young person may express. In response to these negative emotions, adults should avoid retaliation and show an ability to bear frustrations. They also have to realise that it's unreasonable to expect gratitude for having done this! Any negative behaviour directed at an adult may not really be about that adult, though sometimes it can be difficult not to take it personally. The young people's feelings can be transferred to the adult working with them (see section on psychotherapy) and the adult may also experience strong responses to young people because of their own past experiences. Even reading records about the life experiences of some children can emotionally affect the worker, who needs an awareness where the feelings are coming from, and support to process these issues. The adult needs to develop an awareness of his or her responses to the child or young person and what might be causing them. In order to do this, and to be effective, workers need reliable supervision. In this context, supervision as emotional support is most useful (rather than supervision as monitoring), though supervision in order to develop skills and to understand the underlying processes is also beneficial. Supervision should consist of a protected time and space where there is an uncritical dialogue. Attempting to work with young people who have emotional and behavioural difficulties without sufficient support and supervision is likely to lead to burn out and rapid staff turn over, which benefits no one. Support from other team members, rather than competition, is also crucial but often hard to achieve.

Adults can help young people with emotional and behavioural difficulties by being aware of where the strong feelings are coming from and by encouraging the appropriate expression of such emotions. This links to an important psychotherapeutic idea: '…using one's own feelings as a barometer, not only of how one is feeling, but also what is going on for others, what you are picking up from others' (Whitwell 2002, p.101). Modelling clear expressions, of emotions such as 'I feel sad when you talk to him like that', and speculating about other feelings, is valuable. Adults can also teach and model coping behaviours, such as ways to calm down or ways to cheer oneself up when overwhelming emotions occur.

Therefore, the relationship in itself can be as useful as any specific interventions for young people who have difficulties with communicating and with emotions, and this is not incompatible with a professional relationship. If interactions are honest, consistent and trustworthy the young person can learn a lot from them. Friendships with peers and other positive relationships are important for the same reasons and should be nurtured, allowing attachments to develop so the child or young person can develop enough security to become exploratory. Young people with communication and emotional and behavioural difficulties often become socially isolated and exist in a language impoverished environment; therefore interacting with them and making opportunities for others to do so can be beneficial.

Communicating with young people who have communication difficulties

There are particular strategies which can be useful for interacting successfully with young people who have communication difficulties. The communicative style of the person a child interacts with will influence the development of his or her communication skills (Duchan 1989). In order to facilitate language development, it is useful to avoid a directive style. Language development is enhanced if the adult follows the child's focus of interest, gives choices, tries to respond to the child's intent and provides models of communication based on the focus of interest. Accepting children's attempts at communication, while giving feedback about other ways to express themselves, is most helpful. It is important not to 'correct' but to provide models of adult versions in feedback, so if a child says 'He goed', an adult could say, 'Oh, he went, did he?' However, if it were the first time the child had ever put two words together, it would be more appropriate to accept the communication unconditionally (and with much excitement). The type of questions used can also influence how much a young person joins in a conversation; open questions such as 'What do you think about that?' are likely to encourage more of a response than 'Did you like that?'

Young people also benefit when adults try to understand their emotional state in order to respond to it and possibly to discuss it. Calm interventions are best in any emotional situation, alongside an acknowledgement of the feelings being expressed either verbally or non-verbally. Feelings need to be validated; it is acceptable to experience all emotions, but only some ways of expressing them are acceptable (and this will vary from society to society). Young people with communication difficulties, regardless of any other difficulties they may have, often need this kind of emotional support because theirs is an invisible disability.

Given that children and young people with communication problems may have difficulty processing and understanding what they hear, the adult talking with them has a responsibility to consider how they express themselves and to try to make it more accessible. It may be necessary to slow one's rate of speech, and to reduce the length and complexity of sentences. Pausing between phrases will also allow time for processing. Avoiding complex vocabulary and figurative language (such as 'shake a leg' and 'the city ate up the countryside') also enables comprehension. Simple, direct statements are easiest to understand, though they are often rare in adult speech. Recording oneself in conversation will provide insight into how fast and complex most adult speech is. As auditory input may be problematic for a young person with communication difficulties, giving additional visual or kinaesthetic support can be very helpful. Pictures, diagrams, and practical activities, alongside spoken explanations, will often be far more effective than talking alone. In order to overcome comprehension or vocabulary learning difficulties, it is important to repeat key information and concepts often. If someone has attention difficulties, getting their attention before starting to say anything will reduce the number of failed attempts at communication. One can stress the importance of listening by refusing to talk until you are being listened to, but that can take a long time. Adults also have a very important role to play in encouraging young people to say when they don't understand. There are times when we all have difficulty following what someone says, and one can be a good role model for children with difficulty understanding language, by saying so, and asking for clarification.

If children or young people are having difficulty expressing themselves, an adult's focused attention is invaluable. Some children and young people may not be able to use spoken language and will rely on signing or symbols, in which case adults will need a familiarity with the system they are using in addition to the following strategies. Young people with expressive difficulties may simply need more time to formulate and express a response, so patience is the key.

Another important strategy is called expanding; if a child produces a short or incomplete sentence, the adult can respond using the same sentences but expanding it slightly. For example, if the young person says 'He went out, he went to school', the adult could suggest, 'He went out because it was time for school?' It is also possible to model the required language; for example, if someone is getting angry about not being heard, an adult could say, 'Excuse me, can I tell you about it, from my point of view?'. Keeping on topic may also be difficult and adults can help redirect those who wander. Similarly, if a young person gives too much or too little information, this can be pointed out by saying things like 'Yes I saw that' or 'Who are you talking about?' A good relationship between the young person and the adult will enable the adult to know which strategies are likely to be acceptable and when to offer them.

Working together

The importance of collaborative working in order to identify and overcome communicative difficulties in children and young people with complex problems, including behavioural ones, should not be underestimated. Early language, cognitive and emotional development are intertwined; therefore multidisciplinary work is vital if a child experiences difficulties in more than one of these areas. No one has the expertise to understand and help with all of the difficulties a child with such complex special needs faces. Although different strands of child development have often been studied separately, and different professionals have dealt with problems in those areas, it is important to remember that within any child these skills develop simultaneously and the individual may face multiple interacting difficulties with their development. Therefore, in trying to help a young person overcome complex developmental problems, it is vital that different professionals work closely together. It has become particularly clear that working together is necessary to bring about positive change for children with emotional and behavioural difficulties (Cheney 1998).

Teaching skills in isolation can be fruitless; there needs to be a close working relationship with everyone involved with the young person, otherwise new skills, particularly social skills, will not generalise beyond the setting where they were taught. Improving the communicative skills of school-aged children is best done in school, and through the curriculum where possible, although parents and carers still need to be involved (McCartney 1999). Cross *et al.* (2001) and Law and Sivyer (2003) demonstrate the value of different professionals working together, including parents and carers. Working closely with others helps all involved gain a better understanding of what life is like for the young person, and the work is therefore likely to be more effective. Everyone involved in working with a young person with complex problems needs to know their limits and responsibilities, as well as being clear about when they should refer the young person to someone else with more appropriate skills.

Collaboration is not always easy because of the divisive pressures within systems, and because people can feel threatened and undermined by the perceived roles and expectations of others. Negotiation of roles and responsibilities is therefore a crucial part of the process of collaboration. Adults need active learning opportunities to understand each other's roles, as well as support from the organisations they work in, to establish effective working relationships. For collaboration to be successful, everyone has to aim for honest, open communication and to remember that the young person with difficulties should be the main focus (and he or she should always be consulted). Another major barrier to effective teamwork is the considerable shortages of trained professionals in some areas.

Enabling appropriate behaviour

Young people with emotional and behavioural difficulties challenge others and challenge the systems that surround them, including families and schools. Visser (2002) suggests the following possible 'eternal verities' to bear in mind (amongst others) as regards encouraging appropriate behaviour, based on his experience and research:

- Behaviour can change; emotional needs can be met.
- Intervention is second to prevention (in the history of the problem and in each teaching situation).
- Punishment is not as effective as explaining why the behaviour was inappropriate.
- It is important to understand why the behaviour occurs.

Starting with why the behaviour occurs: one factor which is often overlooked, but which is, I would argue, central, is a consideration of the communication skills of any young person with inappropriate behaviour. Improving communication can improve behaviour; for example, in severely handicapped young people, providing functional communication reduces behavioural problems (Johnston and Reichle 1993). Ignoring communication skills, or the lack of them, can render an intervention ineffective, as verbal directives may be meaningless for children with communication difficulties. The language component of intervention programmes for children with emotional and behavioural difficulties should be modified appropriately for children who also have communication problems. Some researchers have also questioned the validity of language-based assessment with this population (Gualtieri *et al.* 1983).

Trying to understand why the behaviour occurs is the first step towards changing it. Unacceptable behaviour expresses young people's needs, emotions and perceptions. If it is possible to meet their needs, and/or distract them from negative behaviours, more positive behaviours can result. Young people's inappropriate behaviour makes sense to them in some way, because they are trying to solve a problem; our job is to help them do that in another way. Careful observation and recording is necessary in order to untangle this. To understand problematic behaviour, it is also often necessary to consider factors beyond the here and now, the way the school, home and family systems interlink, and whether there is good, clear communication between them or not. First it is necessary to consider one's expectations, because inappropriate behaviour doesn't happen in a vacuum:

- Whose problem is this, yours or the young person's?
- Are you being impatient, or expecting too much?
- Is this behaviour really a problem?
- Is this young person trying to communicate something but does not know how?
- Can he (or she) actually do what is being expected of him (or her)? Anyone faced with the impossible will get frustrated and may not behave well as a result.
- What do you want the young person to do instead?

As to challenging behaviours themselves, prevention is the best place to start. Beginnings and endings and indeed any sort of change can be very distressing for young people who have emotional and behavioural difficulties, and confusing for those with communication difficulties, so planning and preparation for such events are vital. There may be certain times of day, or activities, when behaviour difficulties are more likely to occur. This is often in transitions between activities, when it is not clear what everyone should be doing, or when young people have to wait. Therefore, being well organised and keeping young people busy and actively engaged can prevent behaviour problems (Swinson, Woof and Melling 2003).

Children who don't behave well often end up receiving harsh discipline, and then, as they become more coercive, parents give in, reinforcing their behaviour. Therefore, compromising and avoiding head-on conflict is best; some say, 'Only pick a fight you can win.' As regards confrontations, your only choices are to avoid them, give in or escalate and the latter two often lead to unsatisfactory outcomes. Ignore, divert and distract are the first lines of defence. It's always useful to offer a compromise where possible and to allow young people to 'save face'. Often they see their responses as reasonable in the light of others' behaviour. It's also constructive to choose to challenge only the most important misdemeanours – hurting someone can't be ignored, but flicking the desk with a pencil could be. Staying calm and refusing to be drawn into an argument, as well as offering choices to resolve the problem, can de-escalate the situation too. It may also be necessary to reward other young people for ignoring inappropriate behaviour or leaving the scene if necessary.

Boundaries are often discussed with regard to behaviour difficulties. For young people to feel secure, there must be consistent limits to their behaviour, set and reinforced by adults, and those adults must also have clear boundaries to their behaviour. All boundaries will be tested, but if they stand firm they will reassure the young people that the adults will 'look after them' and keep them safe. Boundaries are most effective if they can be developed through negotiation and co-operation, especially as the child gets older. Any rules or expectations must make sense to those who are expected to follow them; there should not be too many of them, they should be positively stated (for example, 'Walk away if you're angry' rather than 'Don't hit Jim'), and they need to be enforceable. Efforts should also be made to help young people understand why rules and boundaries are important. If boundaries are transgressed, clear consequences should result; however, the consequences should preserve the dignity of the transgressors, because if their self-esteem is lowered further it is likely that they will be resentful and less likely to co-operate. Reparation and restitution are important; for example, young people should be encouraged to clear up the mess they made, or to talk to the people they have hurt about how they feel. Incentives are more effective than consequences in encouraging co-operative behaviour, but they will only work if they are things that the young people really want or want to achieve. It is necessary to know them and their interests to motivate them in this way. If they do something a lot, they like it, so observation will give clues to potential positive reinforcers.

Behaviour management programmes are based on the idea that behaviour continues to occur when it is reinforced by a positive consequence. Therefore, to change behaviour you have to understand its 'ABC'; that is, the antecedents, the behaviour itself, and its consequences. If you know what has triggered a particular behaviour it may be possible to remove that trigger, such as a piece of work not making sense to a young person. Alternatively, the consequences of a behaviour may be rewarding to a young person, so if they are changed the behaviour may stop. If a young person climbs up into the rafters after being faced with work that was too difficult, the other students may be amused, and the staff may gather round giving the young person lots of attention, all of which is fun. So altering this consequence might work. The initial stage of behaviour management is a careful assessment of what precipitates the behaviour, so next time something tricky is presented to this student staff can be ready to support the young person in the task, which may prevent the climbing. If not, they can prevent the positive consequences of this behaviour by removing other students to a more interesting location, leaving just one member of staff to monitor the climbing student's safety from a distance, and making it clear that they will only talk to the student once he or she comes down. What complicated the issue is that the antecedents could include earlier negative life experiences, and without an understanding of them it might be difficult to modify current behaviour.

Punishment is not as effective as praise. Punishment breeds a sense of resentment and lowers self-esteem and need not change behaviour. However, if behaviour is inappropriate, sometimes it is useful to remove children briefly from an activity they enjoy, so they come to see that inappropriate behaviour leads to negative consequences. In giving such consequences, one has to be very careful that you are not giving them what they want. Time out from a social situation may be just what communication-impaired children want and they won't see it as negative reinforcement. Also, they need to be in social situations in order to learn how to interact, so removing them has few positive consequences for them. If time out has to be used, then it should involve devising a plan to get back in. Behaviour management regimes may sound simple but they will not work unless there is very careful observation of behaviours first, and a carefully thought out and consistent response to them. Beware of complex explanations of consequences or sanctions; children with communication difficulties may not understand, so it is necessary to keep the language as simple as possible. Some young people will not be able to understand the language and ideas involved in injunctions such as 'If you don't do that writing, you will lose your break', or 'Hit him again and you'll go to bed'. Even if they do understand, they may not have the self-control, the reasoning skills or the ability to look into the future in order to benefit from this kind of approach. This behavioural approach is not one adults readily use on themselves. If things have gone badly and perhaps you didn't behave as well as you should have, will you impose sanctions, or treat yourself to whatever you need to make yourself feel better?

Relying on behavioural management doesn't necessarily encourage young people to think about their behaviour, to learn to solve their own problems, or to take responsibility for their own behaviour. Clearly, they will have to reach a certain developmental level, and acquire some language skills, before this is possible, but it is useful to model problem-solving thinking from an early age. Perhaps the best approach to behavioural difficulties is to teach skills, rather than to try and manage the behaviour alone. For example, saying things such as 'Did throwing the cup get you another drink?' might help young people think about more effective ways to communicate. Then, they may need help with planning a new behaviour, so an adult can suggest, 'If you say "more please", you can have another drink.' It is also important to point out the effects of their behaviours on others (including adults); for example, 'Dan is crying because he's wet. How can we make him feel better?' As children grow older, they benefit from being encouraged to think about how their behaviour is affecting others. Issues such as rights and responsibilities can also be discussed. Those who are the 'victims' of inappropriate behaviour may be able to explain the effect it has had on them, and the class or family can think about ways to solve the problem. Ultimately, it is useful to teach strategies to deal with feelings, ways to stay calm and reasonable, and individualised strategies such as 'When I feel angry I will go and read a book'. Teaching such skills for self-management, self-talk (Audet and Tankersley 1999) and self-monitoring have proven to be effective. Asking young people for problem-solving ideas, or suggestions about how to get on with adults, can draw them into a collaborative problem-solving approach to challenging behaviour.

Self-observation and self-monitoring of positive behaviours often serves to improve behaviour generally; it also raises self-esteem and leads to a growing sense of responsibility. Students (because it has mostly been used in schools) can be given a cue to prompt monitoring, and then they decide if they are achieving their behavioural aim at that point. It may be something such as 'Am I listening?' or 'Am I following instructions?' This sort of self-monitoring can increase attention to task (Lloyd and Hilliard 1989). Students can also monitor and mentor each other as regards the right kinds of interactions.

In trying to deal with difficult behaviour it is important to avoid action without thought, because that is what those behaving inappropriately are doing. Someone wise once said to me, 'They can teach us to be inappropriate quicker than we can teach them to be appropriate.' We need to bear in mind that the only thing we can control in a difficult situation is ourselves and that our responses are important. It is often difficult to find the right approach to inappropriate behaviour so one has to be brave enough to stop doing what isn't working and think again.

'Circle of Friends' (Greenaway 2000) mobilises students to provide a support network for their peers, whatever their difficulties, on the assumption that acceptance leads to change. It recognises the resources that young people have, and their ability to be inclusive. It is easier to hear criticism or suggestions from peers than from people in authority and this kind of approach can lead to more acceptable behaviour.

Widening our knowledge base

Mental health issues, emotional and behavioural problems, and communication difficulties need to be highlighted in the training of all professionals working with young people with complex difficulties, as this is not currently the case. For example, an Ofsted report in 1999 commented that teachers in all kinds of schools need a better understanding of pupils with emotional and behavioural difficulties. Ways should be found for schools and mental health services to work together, perhaps with particular support for schools for young people with emotional and behavioural difficulties, because at present there is little cross-over of expertise.

Furthermore, communication difficulties are often neglected in the training of those who work with young people. Communication difficulties are not always easy to identify, and behaviour indicative of communication problems can be overlooked or misinterpreted. Therefore, everyone working with a child who has emotional and behavioural difficulties (or indeed any children or young people) should receive training about communication problems. An important part of this training would be the identification of communication difficulties, and how assessments of a child or young person's communication skills may be inaccurate if they are based on brief observations in one context. It is also essential for anyone working with a child with emotional, behavioural and communication problems to understand how the latter can have deleterious effects on social and intellectual development. More importantly, it is valuable for people working with communication-impaired children to know how they can help language skills develop. Law *et al.* (2000b), after investigating the provision of services for children with speech and language needs, recommend a comprehensive accredited system of educational and training opportunities for all staff working with children with speech and language needs. This should also include parents and carers. I CAN, a charity for young people with communication difficulties, is developing such a joint training for teachers and speech and language therapists so that they can work together more effectively. Afasic is another charity which champions the rights and needs of young people with communication difficulties and which also provides training. However, there is still a great deal to be done in this area.

Skills to encourage in young people with communication and emotional and behavioural difficulties

Adults can encourage the development of fundamental coping skills in children and young people with complex needs, through providing support or scaffolding while they learn. What young people can do today with help, they can do by themselves tomorrow.

Emotional intelligence

Emotional intelligence is 'the ability to perceive emotions, to access and generate emotions so as to assist thought, to understand emotions and emotional knowledge, and reflectively regulate emotions so as to promote emotional and intellectual growth' (Mayer and Salovey 1997, p.5).

The concept of emotional intelligence is a very useful one because it brings together ideas about emotions, thinking and language. It is important in many real life situations for us to acknowledge that emotions are significant and they can affect how we all behave. Moods bias thoughts (Salovey and Sluyter 1997). Conversely, cognitive behaviour therapy is based on the idea that thoughts (positive or negative) will affect feelings.

The key emotional intelligence skills are as follows:

- knowing how we feel
- knowing how others feel, developing empathy, sympathy
- expressing how we feel
- understanding that emotions aren't always expressed accurately
- coping appropriately with emotional situations
- using emotions to assist thought.

(Saarni 1997)

Many young people with emotional and behavioural problems struggle with knowing how they feel. They need a reliable adult to help them work this out by suggesting labels for their emotions and discussing 'symptoms' of emotions; for example, how anger or sadness lead to sensations in different parts of the body. It can come as a great relief for a young person to realise that we all struggle with difficult feelings at times and that we have various ways of managing them. Anger management training is also based on this kind of thinking (Faupel, Herrick and Sharp 1998). Modelling appropriate ways to express emotions, and providing opportunities to talk about feelings and particularly how to manage them, is essential for the development of emotional intelligence, and this is something that is probably best done in 'real life' situations. However, cooling-off time might be necessary before any thinking about feelings can occur. Discussing feelings will enhance learning the relevant verbal labels, as many young people with emotional and behavioural difficulties, as well as those with communication problems, do not know the words to describe how they are feeling. Through this kind of discussion they can also learn to express negative emotions verbally in ways that are not destructive or unacceptable, and through this they can gain more self-control.

Another important emotional skill is empathy, which can't really develop until there is some self-awareness as regards emotions, and of course theory of mind, which enables one to realise that others can feel the same as us and vice versa. However, considering the emotional effects of events on others can help develop empathy and perspective taking.

Ways to self-soothe or calm oneself are also an important part of emotional intelligence, and these can also be modelled by adults, as can ways to get others to help with calming down. In order to do this, adults need good emotional intelligence skills, because they will have to tune in to the young person's emotional cues, as well as provide models of good emotional intelligence skills.

Reading stories about feelings, and having activities like a worry box (where you put all the things you might need to talk about on slips of paper), all put emotions on the agenda for discussion, and reinforce their significance in everyday life (Novick 1998). The PATHS (Promoting Alternative Thinking Strategies) curriculum (Greenberg *et al.* 1995) is an emotional intelligence curriculum which seems to have had a positive effect on children's development of emotional intelligence skills. Similar work has been carried out successfully with students with moderate learning difficulties in the UK (Lee and Wright 2001).

Self-esteem

Many adolescents with communication difficulties (undetected or not) have become discouraged and alienated. Young people with the label EBD, because of their 'difficult' nature, are unlikely to have had positive interactions with adults or their peers. Adults often have difficulty deciding what these young people can't, or won't, do and they often suffer the consequences of being deemed lazy. These experiences are likely to lead to low self-esteem. Low self-esteem seems to be linked with inappropriate behaviour, poor educational attainment and mental illness. Increasing self-esteem also seems to be a crucial factor in developing resilience against adverse life events. Therefore, raising self-esteem is important in enabling young people with complex difficulties to make progress. If they are to learn new skills and understand themselves better, they have to develop the confidence to try difficult things, and to be willing to make mistakes. They need to believe that, by working hard, they can make progress. Often their experiences have led them to believe the opposite, and often they feel they have no control over whether they succeed or fail, so why try harder? We must also bear in mind that in order to overcome some of the difficulties they face, young people with complex difficulties must put in far more effort than others have to (Licht 1992).

Self-esteem is difficult to define, but it relates to a certain degree of competence and a positive view of oneself. Children tend to believe what adults say (at least when they are young), so what adults say about a young person, and how they say it, is important for their self-image. Ideas about oneself develop from the opinions and reactions of others, so young people who are unable to interact well often receive very little positive feedback. Their self-esteem can be raised by positive feedback and information from others, thereby increasing self-worth. Sometimes the biggest challenge in raising self-esteem is finding positives to give genuine praise for, especially as there needs to be five times as many positive to negative comments for them to have any positive effect. One-to-one attention from a significant adult is important in providing positive feedback. In addition to this, teaching skills that enable the young person to feel competent, such as literacy and social communication skills, are effective in raising self-esteem.

Some of the skills necessary for self-esteem and resilience are to do with problem-solving – having the idea that problems can be resolved or worked on in some way, or even endured if necessary (Werner and Smith 1992). Allowing, encouraging and supporting young people in their attempts to think and problem-solve increases self-esteem and enables them to become independent thinkers.

The following strategies can be effective in raising young people's self-esteem:

- Give positive feedback repeatedly, and frequently; be concrete, specific, honest and accurate – for example, 'You have worked hard at that.' Praise for who they are as well as what they do is also important.

- Catch them doing things right, and remark on it.

- Comment positively on their appearance.

- Remind them of their achievements.

- Set tasks you know they can accomplish, then they know the praise is genuinely earned.

- Comment on your own mistakes in a non-judgemental way; for example, 'I know I can do that right if I try again' rather than 'I'm an idiot'.

- Try to deflect negative comments they or others may make about themselves for example, 'Rubbish is interesting' or 'Dung beetles love that'.

- Earshotting: some young people find it difficult to accept praise directly, so let them overhear you saying something good about them.

- Provide opportunities for them to help others, and then they have something to be proud of.

- Point out their strengths and give opportunities to use them.

- Another important area of self-esteem is pride in one's physical appearance; so new clothes and grooming products can work wonders.

Play

We tend to assume that, given toys, children will play. However, this is not necessarily the case if they haven't had the opportunity or the encouragement to play, or if they are preoccupied with other things; so, they may need help to begin. Many children who have communication difficulties also have delays in the development of play skills. Adults or young people may also think that play is only for children, but this is not so; we can all gain a lot from taking part in activities such as sport, art or drama just for the fun of it, and these are not far removed from the play that children engage in. We can all play with language, with toys and with other people. Playing together is also a good way to develop positive relationships. Adults can help play skills develop by providing opportunities, modelling play, teaching games and by playing *with* children and young people. Apart from the fun to be gained and the energy that can be used up, many skills can be learnt through play. These include physical skills, turn-taking, co-operation, language and emotional skills. In play, scripts and schemas about what people do and say in different situations can be learnt and rehearsed. For example, playing 'doctors' can help a young person understand what usually happens during a visit to a surgery, as well as the vocabulary involved. Through playing with others, young people can explore roles such as being mum or an astronaut, and negotiate events such as who will cook dinner. Encouraging imagining, especially how they could make things better (Novick 1998), can help young people see different possibilities and improve their creative thinking. Play can also be an opportunity to act out daydreams and problem-solve. As a child begins to play symbolically, adults can give a 'running commentary' on their play if the young person is not yet able to do this himself or herself, and this can help develop both language and thinking skills. Suggesting verbal labels for the activities, feelings, needs or beliefs that the child expresses through play is a simple but effective technique. This kind of activity can help develop empathy as well as language skills.

Young people with emotional, behavioural and communication problems may well need support in unstructured play activities; problem behaviours often occur at play time because the skills needed for joining in and negotiating roles are complex. Play is, of course, often an opportunity to be co-operative and to make friends, but this won't happen unless one knows the implicit 'rules' and can join in and take part successfully. Group games can lead to a sense of accomplishment and positive regard for themselves and others while they learn skills, but children and young people with social communication difficulties may need support and to learn specific skills in order to join in. Group games also improve co-operation, especially if they are not competitive, if there is enough structure and if there are group rewards for working together. If adults observe play and keep a record of who played with who, what went well, whether there were any problems and why, then this information can be used to help young people develop the skills they need.

Making friends

Developing a social support network has many benefits, including enhancing self-esteem. Talking with friends helps young people generate more emotional and literal language. Friends also give emotional support, reduce isolation and provide extra resources for problem-solving, so it is worth persevering to develop friendships. This is not necessarily an easy task for young people with emotional, behavioural and communication difficulties; indeed, it may be one of the most difficult things for them to achieve. Therefore, trying to provide opportunities for young people with communication and emotional and behavioural problems to make friends is invaluable as they may find it difficult to create opportunities for themselves.

Some of these young people may need to be taught how to make friends; for example, they may need to be given conversational starters, some ideas about how to approach people, and ways to introduce themselves. There also seem to be 'rules' of friendship which include being reliable, having fun, sharing, trying to resolve conflicts and forgive, talking about yourself and asking questions of others, as well as expressing positive feelings about your friends. These 'rules' can be discussed and encouraged and the specific skills required can be taught. As with developing play skills, semi-structured activities where adults support young people's interactions where necessary are a good first step.

Social problem-solving

Closely related to the skills required to make friends are social problem-solving skills, which are ways to decide how best to respond to others in social situations and to resolve conflicts. Many young people with emotional and behavioural difficulties misunderstand social cues. They may assume that others are being hostile when they are not, so learning to observe and think clearly about what is happening in an encounter can change the way they behave. Systematic problem-solving skills training of this kind has been shown to be effective in increasing positive interactions (Durlak, Fuhrman and Lampman 1991). Social problem-solving skills can also be taught in everyday situations and they can improve the way a young person understands and relates to others. Adults can model the kind of 'self talk' we use to think through difficult situations; eventually the young people will be able to use it for themselves. Seeing this kind of thinking 'in action' can validate it, and empower young people to try it for themselves. It is most effective to teach these skills in real situations as conflict or confusion arises. The thinking and language we use will vary with our cultural experiences but it often includes things like:

- Stop.
- Look and listen for clues.
- What is the problem?
- What are the options for solving it?
- Consider the consequences of each of these.
- Decide what to do.
- Reflect on your choice.

Through working on social problem-solving, young people can develop impulse control, co-operation and ways of settling disputes. Encouraging young people to see things from others' points of view will also help resolve social problems.

An important part of social problem-solving is assertiveness. Often young people who have difficulty with communication, or emotional difficulties, don't realise that they have a right to express their wants, needs, feelings and opinions. Alongside such rights, assertiveness helps them understand that others also have the same rights and that they should be respected.

Narratives

Telling and understanding stories requires emotional, language and thinking skills. Impaired narrative skills are common in children with emotional, behavioural and communication difficulties, and they lead to problems with understanding, remembering and retelling stories as well as with negotiation and problem-solving. Narrative skills are essential for telling each other about our experiences and understanding how events link together in the wider world. Almost everything we say to each other is a story of some kind.

One of the simplest ways to encourage an appreciation of narrative structure is to read stories to a child or young person, particularly if they have literacy difficulties, regardless of their age. Story tapes or CDs are useful for older children, although they obviously don't have the interactive possibilities of story reading. Retelling stories with support, either in play or just through discussing what has been read (or seen on TV), can encourage an understanding of cause and effect. Additionally, retelling will lead to an understanding of the importance of the sequence of events, the emotions involved, and the vocabulary used. Another useful strategy is starting a story and asking a young person to finish it, either verbally or through play.

Before written narratives can develop, there has to be an appreciation and use of narrative structure in speech. It is an understanding of the structure of narratives – that stories need a setting, information about characters, problems and solutions, as well as information about feelings – that enables us to pick out the main points of an event. Without an appreciation of the structure of narrative and its most salient points, a child or young person can be overwhelmed with information when hearing a story. Without an appreciation of the main points it is similarly difficult to begin on constructing a narrative. Once someone has an idea of what should be included in an account, and if they are given time to rehearse their ideas aloud, and to develop a 'plan', then they can begin to construct written narratives. The Communication Opportunity Group Scheme (COGS) (Sage 2002) is a programme which enables children to learn about the different narrative styles expected in class. It does not expect children to write at a level well beyond their expressive language capabilities. De La Paz (2001) also gives examples of how older students can be taught to structure their writing through brainstorming and organising their ideas, then thinking about sentence types and vocabulary as they plan their work.

Social Stories (Gray and Jonker 1994) are a way of helping young people with social communication difficulties (usually those on the autistic continuum) to understand the complexities of a problematic social situation. If their behaviour is unacceptable, or if they find a situation very stressful, a social story about that situation can help young people understand what they need to do to be successful and why. Social Stories are written for the young person after a careful observation of the situation and what is problematic. The stories' visual and static nature can help young people learn relevant social cues and common responses to such a situation, though they may need to read or have the stories read to them many times to achieve this. Such stories are not just a list of instructions, but include information about others' perceptions, feelings and expectations in order to increase understanding of why some ways of behaving are more acceptable than others. Young people who have Asperger's syndrome may be particularly impaired in their ability to social problem-solve (Channon *et al.* 2001) and the social story approach can help them develop the necessary skills.

Specific interventions

In school

In comparison to reading and writing, speaking and listening tend to be neglected in school, though the latter forms the basis for the former. Opportunities for discussion and dialogue are often limited in school, largely due to the demands of the curriculum, and large classes, although it is through dialogue that language skills develop. Not only are language-learning opportunities limited in some schools, but also the language skills required in education are problematic for those with communication difficulties. Many students can hold informal conversations easily enough, but have difficulty with the formal language demands of school. The rules of communication in a classroom are different from those in any other 'conversation'. It is very one-sided: the teacher does most of the talking (teachers talk for three quarters of class time, according to Sage 2000) and he or she controls the interaction. In order to succeed in school, students need to be able to make requests and ask questions in an appropriate manner, and to be able to ask for clarification at the right time and in the right way. (Students with communication difficulties may need to be specifically taught how to ask for clarification and be encouraged to do so.) They also need to know how and when to take a turn, and they must stay on topic and learn a significant amount of new vocabulary and abstract concepts. These skills are often problematic for young people with emotional, behavioural and communication difficulties.

Allowing opportunities for interaction and discussion, and encouraging small group work, can enable less verbal students to say more, feel more able to take risks with thinking, and to learn the necessary social communication skills. Providing activities which encourage students to ask questions, take decisions and problem-solve also enables them to become active, independent learners. Circle Time (Mosley 1996) attempts to redress the balance and give young people more opportunities for discussion and reflection as well as focusing on taking time to listen to children. As a whole school approach based on developing positive relationships, Circle Time can be effective in raising self-esteem, thereby encouraging children to flourish.

Wherever a young person is learning, it will be most effective if their individual learning styles and strengths are taken into account. An assessment of a young person's skills and abilities is vital in giving them appropriate tasks and support, although this can be difficult if students have complex difficulties. Early identification of learning difficulties, often with the help of an educational psychologist, can help develop appropriate learning structures for a young person and reduce the development of emotional difficulties. As we are diverse learners – some learn through seeing, others through doing, others through hearing – input for all the senses will help individual learning styles develop. For example, students with auditory processing difficulties are also likely to need more visual/kinaesthetic support materials (Rinaldi 1996). It is also important to tailor lessons to the attentional skills of students. Some will only be able to concentrate for brief periods, so they will benefit from breaks in learning, frequent changes of activity and opportunities for movement between activities. Ordering activities to allow for a building of learning in gradual steps reduces the frustration of facing a task that is too difficult, and the boredom of one which is not a challenge. Involving the students in this process is also helpful, and then they can see how far they've got towards their targets. In addition to this, allowing students to take part in target setting and selecting the difficulty of their work has been shown to have positive effects on reading (Trenerry 1998). Mediated learning is a way of teaching that encourages students not just to find an answer, but also to think about how they did it. Mediated learning also develops thinking skills, as students are encouraged to think about consequences, and helped to generalise their learning by thinking about other contexts where this type of thing might happen. This kind of directed teaching can overcome the limitations of IQ, and can help students become active learners.

Providing support for pupils during unstructured time, such as playtime and co-operative learning activities, may be necessary to make them positive situations. During these times, the subtle rules of interaction are particularly difficult to fathom because they are unpredictable.

Consider how tiring focusing on structured language-based activities is for someone with communication difficulties (Rinaldi 1996). Students with communication difficulties may need quiet time away from other students when they are tired. It is also most effective to give them instructions relating to possibly problematic, unstructured interactions when they are full of energy. Modifications can also be made to the classroom environment to make it easier for students with emotional, behavioural and communication difficulties. Audet and Tankersley (1999) outline simple ways to alter the physical arrangement of the class, transitions between activities and classes, time structure, and instructional demands in order to make it easier for such students. In a classroom, much can be done by thinking about 'traffic routes' and learning areas; if children have to push past each other between activities there may be trouble. Instructions can be made clearer through direct instruction about what such implicit instructions as 'line up' mean, and by carefully monitoring the appropriateness of linguistic input. It is important to frequently check students' level of understanding, and to make sure vocabulary used is appropriate. It also helps young people understand a task if they are allowed to retell what they have learnt, or if they are encouraged to explain it to others. Where students have difficulty learning language, there needs to be more of an emphasis on teaching core vocabulary; it can't be assumed that they will know these words or be easily able to learn them. Motivating students can be difficult and it is necessary to help them understand the point of what they are being asked to do; for example, by presenting students with aims for each activity, they can appreciate the point of the exercise and what they will learn from it. Students with communication difficulties and emotional and behavioural problems may need extra help seeing the 'bigger picture' – it can't be assumed that it is obvious; it will need to be made explicit.

There are specific strategies that many other students acquire without help which, when made explicit, enable students with difficulties to learn. These include mnemonics, learning key words, chunking information, classification, concept mapping (visual representations of a topic and the factors relevant to it) and other self-organisational skills, such as how to organise work and revise. Teachers and speech and language therapists can work together to help students acquire these skills (Bray 1995; Freedman and Wiig 1995). Students with communication and other difficulties also benefit from help with understanding the different types of narrative structure needed for writing reports, explanations and stories and how to critique them. Explicit teaching of 'life rules' such as being prompt, prepared, participating, showing respect and being responsible (Bodine and Crawford 1999) has also been effective in helping pupils with difficulties succeed in school. The culture of a school affects everyone in it; the level of stress in schools has perhaps been increased by the many changes that have occurred in recent years, and this filters down to the pupils. In addition to the increased organisational demands placed on teachers, they face a difficult task in trying to meet the needs of students who have varying learning styles and abilities. It may be that students with emotional, behavioural and communication difficulties are more sensitive to any negative aspects of schooling, as learning is always an emotional experience, and they often have fewer resources to draw on in order to be tolerant (Cooper 1996). In learning, one is exposing one's ignorance and this is not possible without feeling secure in the situation where learning occurs. Accepting making mistakes as part of the process of learning can help young people make progress; once someone makes a mistake then it's obvious what they need to learn, but this won't happen unless they can be sure of a positive response. Where there is an ethos of high expectations, a sense of community, an acceptance of differences and a feeling that it is acceptable to make mistakes, then all students can thrive. Successful schools tend to have positive expectations of their pupils, and believe in their ability to learn and change; they also tend to have a consultative model of management and a curriculum matched to the pupils' needs. Schools that value personal as well as academic development tend to have higher achieving pupils and fewer behaviour problems (Teale 2000). Schools can do a great deal to raise pupils' self-esteem through rewards such as mentions in assembly, certificates of merit, having work displayed, and outings. Involvement in the running of the school and self-government is also very empowering and through this students learn that with power comes responsibility. The school environment can have a positive effect on EBD students' behaviour (Swinson *et al.* 2003), because behaviour is influenced by external factors such as the way they are taught, as well as factors within the students.

Education is not just something that happens in school, and it is clear that those students who have significant others who value education, and are supportive of teachers, do better. We can all communicate an enthusiasm for learning, and it seems that understanding the value of education is a passport to success. Support for learning and homework and particularly help with reading, all through a young person's school career, has a positive effect. Learning mentors exist in some secondary schools and they aim to help pupils overcome non-educational barriers to learning and provide support for learning.

Speech and language therapists and teachers can successfully collaborate to teach young people who have communication difficulties, but this is less likely to happen outside of specialist provision (such as language units), largely because of staff shortages. Where such collaboration is possible, planning can be done jointly so that vocabulary, thinking skills, narrative and interaction skills are all considered. The aim of this kind of collaboration is to help the student both access the curriculum and to develop their communication skills. Various models of collaboration are used; speech and language therapists may work with students before lessons in order to help them access them, or after, in order to see how well they coped and provide extra input, or lessons might be jointly planned and delivered.

There is an ongoing debate about whether the National Curriculum is sufficient to meet the needs of students with emotional and behavioural, as well as communication, difficulties. They have every right to have access to a broad curriculum, but they may need an additional 'emotional curriculum' as well as special needs teaching where appropriate. The idea of inclusion of students with special needs is laudable. Inclusion does provide opportunities to learn appropriate interaction skills for those with difficulties and for other students to learn from those who are different. However, in practice, teachers are often faced with a large class of students with very disparate abilities, and no additional training or resources to meet the needs of all of those students. Is it a coincidence that in such environments, where there is great emphasis on broad measures of achievement (instead of the fine grained and varied ones necessary to identify the progress some students make), exclusions are on the increase?

Social communication skills

Social communication is often problematic for children and young people who have communication difficulties and/or emotional and behavioural difficulties. However, these skills can be taught and this is best done in groups of peers. The group should take place in a safe and protected time and space (a 'Do not disturb' sign on the door makes this clear). A careful assessment of strengths and weaknesses in social communication skills is necessary in order to identify a baseline. Once this is done, targets can be set in discussion with the young person involved. Whatever the skill or skills are, they have to be clearly defined and broken down. Targets need to be concrete, small and achievable. For example, good listening is generally defined as being still, looking at the speaker and being quiet, and then of course some sort of thinking about what has been said must take place. So a target about improving listening could include any or all of these. Once targets have been defined, the next stage is practising them – perhaps individually, then in gradually larger groups. Role-play is especially helpful here and it can be used to practise before 'real' situations are attempted. Feedback is crucial in learning any new skill. It needs to be accurate and mostly positive. Although negative feedback has to be given at times, it should be done much less frequently and it should be gently done, ideally with humour. Through the modelling of appropriate behaviours, practice in role-play, and good, accurate feedback (ideally using video), young people can change and develop their social communication skills. More sophisticated skills, such as rules of conversation, can also be learnt and students can research this by observing real conversations. 'Scripts' can be developed for starting a conversation or finding out about others, then these can be tried out in role-play, then in real situations. Students can also spend time considering different types of conversations – disputes, retelling stories and problem-solving – and how they differ.

In order to transfer these skills in to real situations, over-learning is often necessary, and an important part of any programme of work on social communication skills is to teach self-evaluation and self-reinforcement. The Social Use of Language Programme (Rinaldi 1992) has useful assessment and activities for this kind of work.

Young people often find this kind of group work difficult, especially if relating to their peers is a major problem for them. Therefore, an understanding of group dynamics and the stages of group development is important for those running the group. It is worth persevering because groups can provide an opportunity to see how powerful communication and being listened to can be. Calling the group 'How to make friends' or 'How to get on well with people' may make it more attractive than the 'Social communication' group.

Group work can be used to develop social problem-solving skills, assertiveness and negotiation skills. When considering social problem-solving, the experiences of group members can be used to generate alternate ways to behave and things to say (to oneself and to others). Also, increasing young people's sensitivity to verbal and non-verbal social cues will help them develop an accurate perception of the problematic situation. Learning 'real life' skills, such as negotiation, can help young people see the value of working together to learn social communication skills. In order to negotiate they need:

- an awareness of the whole situation – the perspectives, feelings and interests of those involved
- to create options for a solution
- to evaluate each option and the effects it might have
- to work towards a win/win solution, where all parties are satisfied with the outcome.

Groups also provide ideal opportunities for fun and playing co-operative group games, which can then be taken into other situations.

Speech and language therapy

Children and young people with communication difficulties should receive specialist help in order to overcome them, so that they can achieve their full potential. Early intervention to develop communication skills may prevent the emergence of behavioural problems, and improved parent–child interaction can reduce abuse (Singer 2000). There is also evidence that programmes that strengthen children's interpersonal language can improve their behavioural functioning (Greenberg *et al.* 1995), and that appropriate interaction skills can be taught and learnt. In addition to this, teaching conversation skills linked to social competence has been shown to improve peer interactions (Bierman and Furman 1984). Also Law and Sivyer (2003) reported speech and language therapy group work with children excluded from school. The students' language, social communication skills and self-esteem were shown to improve as a result of this intervention. Intensive speech and language therapy focused on comprehension and literacy difficulties has also been found to improve secondary school-aged pupils' performance (Leahy and Dodd 2002; Martin-Devins 2001). Speech and language therapy also has an important role in mental health. Unresolved pragmatic difficulties may be a marker for some psychotic illnesses (Muir 1997). Through increasing insight, assertiveness, self-monitoring and self-esteem, people can become more effective, socially appropriate communicators. Jones (1996) also discusses the development of a speech and language therapy service in a child psychiatry setting.

Speech and language therapists can provide information for carers, and for others working with the young person, about the effects of language impairment, as well as specific strategies to overcome it. Increased understanding of communication difficulties can help make interactions more positive. Once adults understand the reasons for the way young people behave, they are less likely to fault them for it. Some young people may be seen as uncooperative, but they may have such difficulty understanding language that they avoid conversations whenever they can. Another child who can't say 'I don't like that, stop it' may bite instead, and once people interacting with the child understand this, they can respond more appropriately and model alternative behaviours. Often it is assumed that children or young people do understand but are not being co-operative, so a speech and language therapy assessment of what they can and cannot understand, both in terms of grammar, vocabulary and abstract language, can be very useful.

Gallagher (1999) suggests that speech and language therapists need to help children with emotional, behavioural and communication problems in the following ways:

- teach communicative alternatives to unacceptable behaviours

- build event-based script knowledge for socially or emotionally difficult situations

- manipulate antecedent behaviours to increase opportunities to practise positive communicative behaviours

- reward socially positive communication behaviours

- develop broader and more varied emotional vocabularies.

Effective speech and language therapy takes into account the young person's strengths, weaknesses, learning style and interests. The approach to therapy itself tends to be eclectic, drawing on research in many fields. Various communication skills may be impaired, and speech and language therapy can help young people develop vocabulary (Foil and Alber 2002), word finding skills (Whitman 1996), grammatical skills, narrative abilities (Gillam *et al.* 1999; Naremore *et al.* 1995), comprehension and sound awareness skills, and an understanding of idiomatic and non-literal language. Using insights about the way language depends on certain cognitive input and output skills, speech and language therapists can also help improve linguistic processing. Psychologists and speech and language therapists teach young people strategies to help overcome memory limitations and to recruit memory strengths. Often simple strategies, such as learning to verbally rehearse in order to remember, can make a big difference. Such skills can then be internalised and used in other situations. There are also computer programmes such as 'Earobics' (available from Cognitive Concepts Inc.), which can improve a child's sound processing skills and have a positive impact on literacy development.

Through speech and language therapy one can encourage the communication of needs, asking questions, asking for clarification and the resolution of differences through stating opinions verbally and negotiating (Johnson 1996). Through collaboration with teaching staff, students with language impairments can be taught strategies which enable them to access a mainstream curriculum more easily (Freedman and Wiig 1995; Wiig 1992).

Group speech and language therapy is often used and is particularly effective for developing social communication skills (Hayden and Pukonen 1996; Paulger 1999). Groups are powerful in encouraging empathy and new patterns of behaviour. They can be used to teach specific interaction skills such as social communication skills, problem-solving and negotiation skills.

Non-directive speech and language therapy has grown out of theories of play therapy; it is essentially providing young people with a running commentary (in appropriate language for them) as they play, without suggesting how they play or what they do. The benefits of this are that the young people are focusing on something while hearing the verbal labels for it, and the lack of direction encourages them to be more exploratory. It can be a useful tool in working with children and young people with emotional and behavioural difficulties, who may not co-operate with more directive activities.

Relaxation techniques often prove very useful for young people who have difficulty managing their emotions. I taught one class some simple relaxation techniques, because one of the students had a stammer and it was useful for him. They all practised relaxation each morning and found it so useful that they also asked their teacher if they could do it at other times, when they felt that their levels of stress were increasing.

Speech and language therapists should bear in mind the possibility that early communication problems may persist and change in nature, so it is difficult to be sure that a child's communication skills are within normal limits and will remain so (Joffe, Doyle and Penn 1996; Stothard et al. 1998). However, given the current organisation of speech and language therapy services, where children often have short periods of therapy, few clinicians are in a position to be able to monitor the progress of children over the long term.

Law et al. (2000b) carried out a survey of services for children with speech and language needs. They found that there is an increasing demand for services for children with communication difficulties, although there is not an increase in provision, and there is particular difficulty with the recruitment and retention of speech and language therapists. Children with EBD, bilingual services and pupils in secondary schools are those most unlikely to receive services. The researchers recommended that services work together and 'that there be a renewed emphasis on the role that speech and language therapy plays in mediating all the child's experiences in school and at home' (p.205). There should also be speech and language therapy services for students in secondary school, as communication difficulties do not disappear as a young person reaches the age of 11 (Botting *et al.* 2001).

Therapeutic interventions

Psychotherapy focuses on the 'inner world' of a child or young person, and is based on the idea that the unconscious mind influences behaviour. Through psychotherapy, change occurs by helping a young person gain insight into the links between current and past events. Therapeutic interventions need to be linked with the whole system of support for a child or young person and not exist in isolation. Psychotherapeutic ideas can also help adults understand children and young people's behaviour, and their own responses to it. Inappropriate behaviour is often an expression of inner conflict and distress linked with how children remember their treatment by adults.

In light of what we know about attachment, it is clear that early experiences can shape thinking, emotional development, and interaction. It is difficult for many of us to understand the impact of attachment disorders – how it feels to have your most fundamental needs unmet – but such experiences can affect interactions for years afterwards. If a young person has been badly treated, that is what they tend to expect. They may also do to others what has been done to them, not necessarily literally, but they can pass on the negative feelings that bad experiences have evoked in them, and in a sense recreate their early experiences. Often young people with emotional and behavioural difficulties may not have had clear, consistent boundaries, and such lack of containment results in an inability to tolerate frustration and muddled thinking, leading to a tendency to just act. Therefore, one psychotherapeutic aim is often to provide containment. Another aim is to offer young people the opportunity to experience the full attention of another person who can respond to them on many levels. The therapeutic space offers safety, boundaries, consistency, authentic responses, trust and spontaneity that result in containment. 'Holding' is a concept that is related to containment, and refers to the child being held emotionally so that they can flourish. It is linked with 'holding in mind', when a child is remembered, and his or her needs and experience are reflected on – it is about keeping the child visible. Young people can also derive security from the containment developed through adults in their network overtly communicating well with each other.

Client-centred therapy is based on unconditional positive regard, genuineness and empathy. The emphasis is on the child's or young person's emotions within this relationship, rather than on any interpretation. The core belief of this and other psychotherapies is that young people have the capacity to grow emotionally; the therapist tries to develop a relationship which helps the young person grow, rather than directing that growth. As psychotherapy is non-directive, it also encourages the young person to be responsible and self-directing; it gives them a sense of control, and self-worth. Psychotherapy is non-judgemental, accepting the young person though not necessarily their behaviour. A relationship of trust is vital or the young person may not be able to begin on the difficult work of thinking about themselves.

Transference is the term for the unconscious projection of one's feelings onto someone else; according to psychodynamic theory, all interpersonal relationships can be distorted by transference. Theories about why individual children behave the way they do are therefore far from objective. Our experiences shape the way we relate to others and it is important to try and understand this, particularly in a relationship with a 'difficult' child. The young person may project his or her disturbance on to others, making them the target of the hurt and confusion. This can make these people feel as hurt and confused as the young person does, unless they understand what this transference of emotion is. The adults in a situation like this need to be able to survive this onslaught, and then try to help the young person understand what is going on. It is implicit in this that it is important for the adults to understand as much as possible about their own inner lives, in order to recognise when something in their past interferes with their interactions with young people. One might respond to a child behaving inappropriately in one way because they remind you of someone you loved, and in another if they are like someone you hated. Whether or not a young person receives psychotherapy, consultation with a psychotherapist can help others in their understanding and management of a child or young person whose behaviour is confusing (Weiss 2002).

One of the aims of psychotherapy is to help young people to symbolise, or think about, what they're experiencing, and clearly a large part of this will be through language. 'Symbolisation or mentalisation can be seen as a means of creating a psychic skin' (James 2002, p.194) over emotional wounds. It is important for everyone involved to try to understand what the behaviour means; it is a communication of some kind. It may take time and the help of others to decode the behaviour and for the young person to learn to express the underlying feelings in another way. Psychotherapeutic techniques help develop emotional and communication skills, as children can learn self-regulation by thinking about emotions in a safe relationship (Osofsky, Cohen and Drell 1995).

Defences – such as repression, denial, regression, rationalisation and projection (attributing unacceptable feelings to others) – against expressing overwhelming feelings allow a young person to manage in the short term but they can disguise feelings and block progress. Psychotherapeutic theory enables an understanding of such defences, and provides an environment that can help the young person understand them as well and begin to find ways to express their true feelings.

Play therapy is a form of psychotherapy which uses play to help the development of symbolisation. It is particularly useful for those who are unable, for various reasons, to put their feelings into words. The use of symbols helps young people express things that they can't define or fully represent. There are books for children about this including *The Special Playroom: A Young Child's Guide to Play Therapy* (Gilfix and Kahn 1999).

Systemic theory helps us understand how we function in the context of families and/or organisations. The family is an interactive and interdependent system, and it is often a mistake to focus on the individual who has the 'symptoms', because they are part of a system that influences their behaviour, and that behaviour serves a function for the family. For example, families who have children with very difficult behaviour tend to have defensive communications, blame each other more, and tend not to support one another. Therefore, the goal of family therapy is to improve communication and mutual support by helping family members see the 'problem' from other points of view. Multisytemic therapy, which considers other systems the child is part of, as well as the family, has been shown to be effective in improving behaviour in adolescents (Henggeler *et al.* 1998).

Solution-focused brief therapy is, as the title suggests, a focus on solutions rather than problems. It assumes that everyone has the resources they need to succeed, and it tries to focus on these rather than on problems. So, instead of the problem, young people are encouraged to think about what they would like to be doing instead, and do it. This approach has proved useful in schools (Rhodes and Ajmal 1995).

How can young people access a 'talking therapy' if they have difficulty with communication? Stacey (1995) considers ways in which family therapists can enable language-impaired children to access the language of therapy. She suggests using concrete explanations, using analogy rather than metaphor and rephrasing or acting out questions. She considers this to be vital in order to include their ideas and not marginalise them in therapy. Psychotherapy has been shown to have a positive effect on language development (Russell, Greenwald and Shirk 1991), probably because the children experience individual attention and responsiveness that clarifies and expands on what they are trying to communicate.

Research and evaluation

Little is known about which are the most effective interventions for children with communication difficulties and emotional and behavioural difficulties, but despite this, positive outcome measures are often vital in the current climate in order to get funding for intervention. So there is a great need for research in this area. Since communication, learning and emotional difficulties all co-exist within some children and young people, they need comprehensive and integrated service delivery regardless of aetiology or which is the primary disability (Rock *et al.* 1997). The complex learning, language and behavioural disorders in children with emotional and behavioural problems underscore the importance of teamwork and integration of services, if the children and young people are to receive the help they need (Thomas, Corea and Morsink 1995). It is also likely that long-term services will be necessary in order to make a difference to young people with such complex interrelated difficulties.

Conclusion

There is much that can be done to help young people with emotional, behavioural and communication difficulties, but in order for these to occur some major organisational changes are necessary:

- It should not be forgotten that communication difficulties are not always identified, especially when the child or young person also has emotional and behavioural difficulties, and that communication difficulties can have negative effects on their development.

- Children and young people with emotional and behavioural difficulties should therefore be screened for communication difficulties (Benner, *et al.* 2002) (in particular those who are suspected of having been mistreated emotionally, physically or sexually).

- Young people with communication difficulties also should be screened for emotional and behavioural difficulties.

- Early intervention for emotionally disturbed children should address language deficits.

- Speech and language therapists should be involved in designing intervention programmes for children with emotional and behavioural difficulties.

- Speech and language therapy should be available for children with emotional and behavioural difficulties, including those who have been excluded from school and those who are in secondary school.

- Professionals need to be able to recognise the difference between non-compliance and not understanding, and the difference between non-verbal communication and aggression.

- Information on a child's ability to communicate is crucial and should be part of the records which accompany a child to any new school or foster care placement.

- Measurement of a child or young person's communication skill development while in public care might give an indication of the effectiveness of the placement.

✓

Indicators list for identifying communication problems

Young person's name:
Date of Birth:
Completed by: **Date:**

Have you observed any of the following?

Form

- Speaks too quickly (i.e. words run into each other)   ☐
- Is not easily understood   ☐
- Uses unusual or awkward grammar   ☐
- Says the same word differently at different times   ☐
- Stammers (e.g. hesitates, repeats sounds/words, gets stuck)   ☐
- Has problems with prepositions (e.g. on, under, over, behind) or tenses   ☐
- May take a long time to organise words into a sentence   ☐
- Misses out words or puts them in the wrong order   ☐
- Has problems giving specific answers or explanations   ☐
- Has difficulties joining sentences with 'and', 'because', 'so', etc. or uses one of these words too much   ☐
- Has problems sequencing events and ideas appropriately   ☐
- Cannot retell a simple story   ☐

Content

- Has limited vocabulary, which could lead to excessive swearing   ☐
- Finds it hard to express emotions verbally   ☐

- Has fluent, clear speech which doesn't seem to mean much ☐
- Has trouble learning new words (e.g. names of people and objects) ☐
- Fails to provide significant information to listeners ☐
- Uses made-up words which are almost appropriate (e.g. 'window worker man') ☐
- Overuses certain 'meaningless' words (e.g. 'thingy', 'whatever', 'and that' etc.) ☐

Using language with others

- Interrupts inappropriately ☐
- Avoids situations which require words ☐
- Is unable to vary language with the situation ☐
- Attracts attention in inappropriate ways or without words ☐
- In conversation moves from topic to topic for no obvious reason or finds it difficult to change the subject ☐
- Has problems taking turns in conversation ☐
- Doesn't ask questions or start a conversation ☐
- Doesn't say if unable to understand ☐

Understanding language

- Has difficulties following long or complex instructions ☐
- Has better understanding in a 1:1 situation than in a group ☐
- Watches and copies others when instructions are given ☐
- Is unable to remember and recount last week's episode of a 'soap' on TV ☐
- Tends to take things literally ☐
- Doesn't understand sentences with 'if', 'when', 'so' etc. ☐
- Responds inappropriately to abstract language (e.g. 'keep your hair on') ☐
- Repeats what you say rather than responding appropriately ☐
- Has problems understanding implied meanings (e.g. 'I wouldn't take my shoes off now' meaning 'Don't take your shoes off') ☐
- Is slow to learn new routines ☐

APPENDIX 2

Useful organisations

Afasic
2nd Floor
50–52 Great Sutton Street
London EC1V 0DJ
website: www.afasic.org.uk

The American Speech-Language-Hearing Association (ASHA)
website: www.asha.org

The Association for Child Psychology and Psychiatry
St Saviours House
39/41 Union St
London SE1 1SD
website: www.acpp.org.uk

**The Association of Workers for Children with Emotional
and Behavioural Difficulties**
Secretary: Sue Panter
20 Carlton Street
Kettering
Northants NN16 8EB
website: www.awcebd.co.uk

BAAF Adoption and Fostering
Skyline House
200 Union Street
London SE1 0LX
website: www.baaf.org.uk

I CAN
4 Dyer's Buildings
Holborn
London EC1N 2QP
website: www.ican.org.uk

The Royal College of Speech and Language Therapists
2 White Hart Yard
London SE1 1NX
website: www.rcslt.org

References

Abkarian, G. G. (1992) 'Communication effects of prenatal alcohol exposure.' *Journal of Communication Disorders 25*, 4, 221–240.

Achenbach, T. M. (1991) *Manual for the Child Behaviour Checklist 4–18.* Burlington, VT: University of Vermont Press.

Ackerman, B. (1982) 'On comprehending idioms: do children get the picture?' *Journal of Experimental Psychology 33*, 439–454.

Adcock, M. and White, R. (eds) (1998) *Significant Harm: Its Management and Outcome.* London: Significant Publications.

Afasic (2003) *How to Identify and Support Children with S and L Difficulties.* London: LDA.

Ainsworth, M. D. S., Blehar, M., Waters, E. and Wall, S. (1978) *Patterns of Attachment: A Psychological Study of the Strange Situation.* Hillsdale, NJ: Lawrence Erlbaum.

Alderson, P. (1995) *Listening to Children: Children, Ethics and Social Research.* London: Barnardo's.

Aldgate, J., Heath, A., Colton, M. and Simm, M. (1993) 'Social work and the education of children in foster care.' *Adoption and Fostering 17*, 3, 25–35.

Allen, R. and Wasserman, A. (1985) 'Origins of language delay in abused infants.' *Child Abuse and Neglect 9*, 335–340.

American Psychiatric Association (1994) *Diagnostic and Statistical Manual of Mental Disorders, 4th edition* (DSM-IV). Washington, DC: American Psychiatric Association.

Anderson, J. C., Williams, S., McGee, R. and Silva, P. A. (1987) 'DSM-III-R disorders in preadolescent children: prevalence in a large sample from the general population.' *Archives of General Psychiatry 44*, 69–76.

Anderson-Wood, L. and Smith, B. R. (1997) *Working with Pragmatics: A Practical Guide to Promoting Communicative Confidence.* Bicester: Winslow Press Ltd.

Andreason, N. C. (1979) 'Thought, language and communication disorders: 1. Definition of terms and their reliability.' *Archives of General Psychiatry 36*, 12, 1315–1321.

Aram, D. M., Hack, M., Hawkins, S., Weissman, B. M. and Borawski-Clark, E. (1991) 'Very low birth weight children and speech and language development.' *Journal of Speech and Hearing Research 34*, 1169–1179.

Aram, D. M., Morris, R. and Hall, N. E. (1993) 'Clinical and research congruence in identifying children with specific language impairment.' *Journal of Speech and Hearing Research 36*, 580–591.

Asher, S. R. and Gazelle, H. (1999) 'Loneliness, peer relations, and language disorder in childhood.' *Topics in Language Disorders 19*, 2, 16–33.

Audet, L. R. and Tankersley, M. (1999) 'Implications of communication and behavioural disorders for classroom management: collaborative intervention techniques.' In D. Rogers-Adkinson and P. Griffith (eds) *Communication Disorders and Children with Psychiatric and Behavioural Disorders.* San Diego and London: Singular Publishing Group Inc.

Bailey, P. J. and Snowling, M. J. (2002) 'Auditory processing and the development of language and literacy.' *British Medical Bulletin 63*, 135–146.

Baker, L. and Cantwell, D. P. (1987) 'A prospective psychiatric follow-up of children with speech and language disorders.' *Journal of the American Academy of Child and Adolescent Psychiatry 26*, 546–553.

Baltaxe, C. A. M. and Simmons, J. Q. (1988a) 'Communication deficits in pre-school children with psychiatric disorders.' *Seminars in Speech and Language 9*, 81–91.

Baltaxe, C. A. M. and Simmons, J. Q. (1988b) 'Pragmatic deficits in emotionally disturbed children and adolescents.' In R. Scheifelbusch and L. L. Lloyd (eds) *Language Perspectives: Acquisition, Retardation and Intervention.* 2nd Edn. Austin, TX: Pro-Ed.

Baltaxe, C. A. M. and Simmons, J. Q. (1995) 'Speech and language disorders in children and adolescents with schizophrenia.' *Schizophrenia Bulletin 21,* 4, 677–692.

Bamford, F. and Wolkind, S. N. (1988) *The Physical and Mental Health of Children in Care: Research Needs.* London: Economic and Research Council.

Barden, R. C., Ford, M. E., Jensen, A. G., Rogers-Salyer, M. and Salyer, K. E. (1989) 'Effects of craniofacial deformity in infancy on the quality of mother–infant interactions.' *Child Development 60,* 819–824.

Barkley, R. A. (1994) 'Delayed responding and attention deficit hyperactivity disorder: a unified theory.' In D. K. Routh (ed) *Disruptive Behavior Disorders in Children: Essays in Honor of Herbert Quay.* New York: Plenum Press.

Barkley, R. A. (1997) 'Behavioural inhibition, sustained attention and executive functions: constructing a unifying theory of ADHD.' *Psychological Bulletin 121,* 65–94.

Barnett, D. W., Carey, K. T. and Hall, J. D. (1993) 'Naturalistic intervention design for young children: foundations, rationales, and strategies.' *Topics in Early Childhood Special Education 13,* 430–444.

Baron-Cohen, S. (1995) *Mindblindness.* Cambridge, MA: MIT Press.

Bashir, A., Kuban, K., Kelinman, S. and Scavuzzo, S. (1983) 'Issues in language disorders: considerations of cause, maintenance and change.' In J. Miller, D. Yoder and R. Schiefelbush (eds) *ASHA Report No.12.* Rockville, MD: American Speech-Language-Hearing Association.

Bates, E. and McWhinney, B. (1987) 'Competition, variation and language learning.' In B. McWhinney (ed) *Mechanisms of Language Learning.* Hillsdale, NJ: Lawrence Erlbaum.

Bates, E., Dale, P. and Thal, D. (1995) 'Individual differences and their implications for theories of language development.' In P. Fletcher and B. McWhinney (eds) *The Handbook of Child Language.* Oxford: Basil Blackwell.

Bates, E., Thal, D. and Janowsky, J. S. (1992) 'Early language development and its neural correlates.' In S. J. Segalowitz and I. Rapin (eds) *Handbook of Neuropsychology 7.* Amsterdam: Elsevier.

Bax, M. (1983) 'Editorial: child abuse and cerebral palsy.' *Developmental Medicine and Child Neurology 25,* 141–142.

Beals, D. E., De Temple, J. M. and Dickinson D. K. (1994) 'Talking and listening that support early literacy development of children from low-income families.' In D. K. Dickinson (ed) *Bridges to Literacy: Children, Families and Schools.* Cambridge, MA: Blackwell.

Beitchman, J. H. (1985) 'Speech and language impairment and psychiatric risk: toward a model of neurodevelopmental immaturity.' *Psychiatric Clinics of North America 8,* 721–735.

Beitchman, J. H., Hood, J., Rochon, J. and Peterson, M. (1989) 'Empirical classification of speech/language impairment in children: II. Behavioural characteristics.' *Journal of the American Academy of Child and Adolescent Psychiatry 32,* 585–594.

Beitchman, J. H., Wilson, B., Brownlie, E. B., Walters, H., Inglis, A. and Lancee, W. (1996) 'Long-term consistency in speech/language profiles: II. Behavioural, emotional and social outcomes.' *Journal of the American Academy of Adolescent Psychiatry 35,* 6, 804–814.

Benasich, A. A., Curtiss, S. and Tallal, P. (1993) 'Language, learning and behavioural disturbances in childhood: a longitudinal perspective.' *Journal of the American Academy of Child Psychiatry 31,* 3, 585–594.

Benner, G. J., Nelson, R. and Epstein, M. H. (2002) 'Language skills of children with EBD: a literature review.' *Journal of Emotional and Behavioural Disorders 10,* 1, 43–59.

Berk, L. and Landau, S. (1993) 'Private speech of learning disabled and normally achieving children in classroom, academic and laboratory context.' *Child Development 64,* 556–571.

Biehal, N., Calyden, J., Stein, M. and Wade, J. (1995) *Moving On: Young People and Leaving Care Schemes.* London: HMSO.

Bierman, K. L. and Furman, W. (1984) 'The effects of social skills training and peer involvement on the social adjustment of preadolescents.' *Child Development 55*, 151–162.

Bishop, D. V. M. (1992) 'The underlying nature of specific language impairment.' *Journal of Child Psychology and Psychiatry 33*, 3–66.

Bishop, D. V. M. (1998) 'Development of the Children's Communicative Checklist (CCC): a method for assessing qualitative aspects of communicative impairment in children.' *Journal of Child Psychology and Psychiatry 39*, 6, 879–891.

Bishop, D. V. M., North, T. and Donlan, C. (1996) 'Nonword repetition as a behavioural marker for inherited language impairment: evidence from a twin study.' *Journal of Child Psychology and Psychiatry 36*, 1–13.

Blager, F. B. (1979) 'The effect of intervention on speech and language of abused children.' *Child Abuse and Neglect 5*, 991–996.

Bloom, L. and Beckwith, R. (1989) 'Talking with feeling: integrating affective and linguistic expression in early language development.' *Cognition and Emotion 3*, 313–342.

Bloomquist, M., August, G., Cohen, C., Doyle, A. and Everhart, K. (1997) 'Social problem solving in hyperactive-aggressive children: how and what they think in conditions of automatic and controlled processing.' *Journal of Clinical Child Psychology 26*, 2, 172–180.

Bodine, R. J. and Crawford, D. K. (1999) *Developing Emotional Intelligence: A Guide to Behaviour Management and Conflict Resolution in Schools.* Illinois: Research Press.

Bonitatibus, G. (1988) 'Comprehension monitoring and the apprehension of literal meaning.' *Child Development 59*, 60–70.

Botting, N. and Conti-Ramsden, G. (2000) 'Social and behavioural difficulties in children with language impairment.' *Child Language Teaching and Therapy 16*, 2, 105–120.

Botting, N., Faraghjer, B., Simkin, Z., Knox, E. and Conti-Ramsden, G. (2001) 'Predicting pathways of specific language impairment: what differentiates good and poor outcome?' *Journal of Child Psychology and Psychiatry 42*, 8, 1013–1020.

Bradshaw, J. L. (2002) *Developmental Disorders of the Frontostriatal System: Neuropsychological, Neuropsychiatric and Evolutionary Perspectives.* London: Taylor and Francis.

Bray, C. M. (1995) 'Developing study, organisation and management strategies for adolescents with language disabilities.' *Seminars in Speech and Language 16*, 1, 65–83.

Brestan, E. V. and Eyeberg, S. M. (1998) 'Effective psychosocial treatment of conduct-disordered children and adolescents: 29 years, 82 studies and 5275 kids.' *Journal of Clinical Child Psychology 55*, 311–318.

Bretherton, I., Fritz, J., Zahn-Waxler, C. and Ridgeway, D. (1986) 'Learning to talk about emotions: a functionalist perspective.' *Child Development 57*, 529–584.

Bricklin, P. M. and Gallico, R. (1984) 'Learning disabilities and emotional disturbance: critical issues in definition, assessment and service delivery.' *Learning Disabilities 3*, 12, 141–156.

Brinton, B., Fujiki, M. and Higbee, L. (1998) 'Participation in cooperative learning activities by children with SLI.' *Journal of Speech, Language and Hearing Research 41*, 1193–1206.

Brown, J. R. and Donelan-McCall, N. (1993) 'Talk with your mother or your siblings? Developmental changes in early family conversations about feelings.' *Child Development 63*, 336–349.

Bruner, J. S. (1983) *Child's Talk: Learning to Use Language.* New York: Norton.

Buitelaar, J. K., Swinkels, H. N., de Vries, H., van der Gaag, R. J. and van Hoof, J. A. R. A. M. (1994) 'An ethological study on behavioural differences between hyperactive, aggressive, combined hyperactive/aggressive and control children.' *Journal of Child Psychology and Psychiatry 35*, 8, 1437–1446.

Burden, V., Stott, C. M., Forgr, J. and Goodyer, I. (1996) 'The Cambridge Language and Special Project (CLASP): 1. Detection of language difficulties at 36–39 months.' *Developmental Medicine and Child Neurology 38*, 613–631.

Burgess, J. and Bransby, G. (1990) 'An evaluation of the speech and language skills of children with emotional and behavioural problems.' *College of Speech Therapy Bulletin 453*, 2–3.

Butler, I. and Payne, H. (1997) 'The health of children looked after by the Local Authority.' *Adoption and Fostering 21*, 2, 1–14.

Butler, I. and Williamson, H. (1994) *Children Speak, Children Trauma and Social Work*. London: Longman.

Camarata, S., Hughes, C. and Ruhl, K. (1988) 'Mild/moderate behaviourally disordered students: a population at risk for language disorders.' *Language, Speech and Hearing Services in Schools 19*, 191–200.

Campbell, T. F., Dollaghan, C., Needleman, H. and Janosky, J. (1997) 'Reducing bias in language assessment: processing dependent measures.' *Journal of Speech, Language and Hearing Research 40*, 519–529.

Cannon, M., Caspi, A., Moffitt, T. E., Harrington, H., Taylor, A., Murray, R. M. and Poulton, R. (2002) 'Evidence for early-childhood pan-developmental impairment specific to schizophreniform disorder: results from a longitudinal birth cohort.' *Archives of General Psychiatry 59*, 5, 449–457.

Cantwell, D. P. and Baker, L. (1991) 'Association between attention deficit-hyperactivity disorder and learning disorders.' *Journal of Learning Disabilities 24*, 2, 88–95.

Caplan, R. (1996) 'Discourse deficits in childhood schizophrenia.' In J. M. Beitchman (ed) *Language Learning and Behaviour Disorders: Developmental, Biological and Clinical Perspectives*. New York: Cambridge University Press.

Caulfield, M. B. (1989) 'Communication difficulty: a model for the relation of language delay and behaviour problems.' *Society for Research in Child Development Abstracts 7*, 212.

Champagne, S. and Cronk, C. (1998) 'Le mutisme sélectif étudié à travers l'expérience d'un échantillon d'orthophonistes Québécois. Fréquences.' *Canadian Association of Speech Language Pathologist Journal, Quebec 10*, 4, 23–26.

Channon, S., Charman, T., Heap, J., Crawford, S. and Rios, P. (2001) 'Real-life-type problem-solving in Asperger's Syndrome.' *Journal of Autism and Developmental Disorders 31*, 5, 461–469.

Cheney, R. (1998) 'Using action research as a collaborative process to enhance educators' and families' knowledge and skills for youth with emotional or behavioural disorders.' *Preventing School Failure 42*, 2, 88–93.

Chernoff, R., Combs-Orme, T., Risley-Curtiss, C. and Heisler, A. (1994) 'Assessing the health status of children entering foster care.' *Pediatrics 93*, 594–601.

Cicchetti, D. and Beeghly, M. (1987) 'Symbolic development in maltreated youngsters: an organizational perspective.' *New Directions for Child Development 36*, 47–68.

Clegg, J., Hollis, C. and Rutter, M. (1999) 'Life sentence.' *Royal College of Speech and Language Therapists Bulletin*, November, 571, 16–18.

Cline, T. and Baldwin, S. (1994) *Selective Mutism in Children*. London: Whurr.

Cloward, R. A. and Ohlin, L. E. (1960) *Delinquency and Opportunity: A Theory of Delinquent Gangs*. New York: Free Press.

Cohen, N. J. (1992) 'Psychiatrically disturbed children with unsuspected language impairments: developmental differences in language and behavioural characteristics.' Paper presented at the conference Integrating Language Learning and Behaviour: Theory and Applications, Toronto, Canada (May).

Cohen, N. J. and Lipsett, L. (1991) 'Recognised and unrecognised language impairment in psychologically disturbed children. Child symptomatology, maternal depression and family dysfunction.' *Canadian Journal of Behavioural Science 23*, 3, 376–389.

Cohen, N. J., Barwick, M. A., Horodezky, N. B., Vallance, D. D. and Im, N. (1998a) 'Language, achievement, and cognitive processing in psychiatrically disturbed children with previously identified and unsuspected language impairments.' *Journal of Child Psychology and Psychiatry 39*, 6, 865–877.

Cohen, N. J., Davine, M., Horodezky, N.B., Lipsett, L. and Isaacson, B. A. (1993) 'Unsuspected language impairments in psychiatrically disturbed children: prevalence and language and behavioural characteristics.' *Journal of the American Academy of Child and Adolescent Psychiatry 32*, 595–603.

Cohen, N. J., Menna, R., Vallance, D. D., Barwick, M. A., Im, N. and Horodezky, N. B. (1998b) 'Language, social cognitive processing, and behavioural characteristics of psychiatrically disturbed children with previously identified and unsuspected language impairments.' *Journal of Child Psychology and Psychiatry 39*, 6, 853–864.

Conti-Ramsden, G., Crutchley, A. and Botting, N. (1997) 'The extent to which psychometric tests differentiate subgroups of children with SLI.' *Journal of Speech, Language and Hearing Research 40*, 765–777.

Cook, E. T., Greenberg, M. T. and Kusche, C. A. (1994) 'The relationships between emotional understanding, intellectual functioning and disruptive behaviour in elementary school-aged children.' *Journal of Abnormal Child Psychology 22*, 205–220.

Cooper, P. (1996) 'The inner life of children with emotional and behavioural difficulties.' In V. P. Varma (ed) *The Inner Life of Children with Special Needs.* London: Whurr Publishers.

Coster, W. and Cicchetti, D. (1993) 'Research on the communicative development of maltreated children: clinical implications.' *Topics in Language Disorders 13*, 4, 25–38.

Council for Learning Disabilities (1986) 'Use of discrepancy formulas in the identification of learning disabled individuals.' *Learning Disability Quarterly 9*, 245.

Crittenden, P. M. (1995) 'Attachment and psychopathology.' In S. Goldberg, R. Muir and J. Kerr (eds) *Attachment Theory: Social, Developmental and Clinical Perspectives.* Hillsdale, NJ: The Analytic Press.

Cross, M. (1999) 'Lost for words.' *Child and Family Social Work 42*, 249–257.

Cross, M. (2001) 'Undetected communication problems in children who are looked after by the local authority.' Unpublished MPhil thesis, Cardiff University.

Cross, M., Blake, P., Tunbridge, N. and Gill, T. (2001) 'Collaborative working to promote the communication skills of a 14-year-old student with emotional, behavioural, learning and language difficulties.' *Child Language Teaching and Therapy 17*, 3, 227–246.

Dale, P. S. (1996) 'Language and emotion: a developmental perspective.' In J. H. Beitchman and N. J. Cohen (eds) *Language, Learning, and Behavior Disorders: Developmental, Biological, and Clinical Perspectives.* New York: Cambridge University Press.

Davison, F. M. and Howlin, P. (1997) 'A follow-up study of children attending a primary age language unit.' *European Journal of Disorders of Communication 32*, 19–36.

De La Paz, S. (2001) 'Teaching writing to students with attention deficit disorders and specific language impairment.' *Journal of Educational Research 95*, 1, 37–47.

De Rosnay, M. and Harris, P. L. (2002) 'Individual differences in children's understanding of emotion: the roles of attachment and language.' *Attachment and Human Development 4*, 1, 39–54.

Department for Education and Skills (2001a) *Draft Revised Code of Practice for the Identification and Assessment of Special Educational Needs.* London: Department for Education and Skills. www.dfes.gov.uk

Department for Education and Skills (2001b) *Special Educational Needs Code of Practice.* www.dfes.gov.uk/sen/

Department for Education and Skills/Department of Health (2000) *The Education of Children and Young People in Public Care.* London: DFES.

Department of Health (1991a) *The Children Act 1989 Guidance and Regulation, Vol. 3. Family Placements.* London: HMSO. www.doh.gov.uk

Department of Health (1991b) *Looking after Children: A Guide to Action and Assessment Schedules.* London: HMSO. www.doh.gov.uk

Department of Health (1995) *Looking After Children, Assessment and Action Records.* London: HMSO. www.doh.gov.uk

Department of Health (1998) LAC (98) 28. *The Quality Protects Programme: Transforming Children's Services.* www.doh.gov.uk

Department of Health (1999) *The Government's Objectives for Children's Social Services.* A *Quality Protects* Publication. www.doh.gov.uk

Department of Health/Department for Education and Employment/Home Office (2000) *Framework for the Assessment of Children in Need and their Families.* London: The Stationery Office. www.doh.gov.uk

Department of Health and Social Security (1985) Social Work Decisions in Child Care: Research Findings and Their Implications. London: HMSO.

Dixon, W. E. and Smith, P. H. (2000) 'Links between early temperament and language acquisition.' *Merril-Palmer Quarterly 46*, 3, 417–440.

Dockrell, J., George, R., Lindsay, G. and Roux, J. (1997) 'Problems in the identification and assessment of children with specific speech and language difficulties.' *Educational Psychology in Practice 13*, 1, 29–38.

Dollaghan, C. and Campbell, T. F. (1998) 'Nonword repetition and child language impairment.' *Journal of Speech, Language and Hearing Research 41*, 1136–1146.

Dubowitz, H., Fengelmen, S., Tepper, V., Sawyer, R. and Darylson, N. (1990) *The Physical and Mental Health and Educational Status of Children Placed with Relatives: Final Report.* Baltimore, MD: University of Maryland Medical School, Department of Pediatrics.

Duchan, J. (1989) 'Evaluating adults' talk to children: assessing adult attunement.' *Seminars in Speech and Language 10*, 17–27.

Dunkin, J. and Biddle, B. (1974) *The Study of Teaching.* New York: Holt, Rinehart and Winston.

Dunn, M., Flax, J., Sliwinski, M. and Aram, D. (1996) 'The use of spontaneous language measures as criteria for identifying children with specific language impairment: an attempt to reconcile clinical and research incongruence.' *Journal of Speech and Hearing Research 39*, 3, 643–654.

Durlak, K. A., Fuhrman, T. and Lampman, C. (1991) 'Effectiveness of cognitive behavior therapy for maladapting children: a meta-analysis.' *Psychological Bulletin 110*, 204–214.

Fabes, R. A., Eisenberg, N., Hanish, L. D. and Spinrad, T. L. (2001) 'Preschoolers' spontaneous emotion vocabulary: relations to likability.' *Early Education and Development 12*, 11–27.

Fahlberg, V. (1981) *Attachment and Separation.* London: British Agencies for Adoption and Fostering (BAAF).

Farrell, P. and Tsakalidou, K. (1999) 'Recent trends in the re-integration of pupils with emotional and behavioural difficulties in the United Kingdom.' *School Psychology International 20*, 4, 323–327.

Farrell, P., Critchley, C. and Mills, C. (1999) 'The educational attainments of pupils with emotional and behavioural difficulties.' *British Journal of Special Education 26*, 1, 50–53.

Faupel, A. Herrick, E. and Sharp, P. M. (1998) *Anger Management: A Practical Guide.* London: David Fulton.

Felsenfeld, S. and Plomin, R. (1997) 'Epidemiological and offspring analyses of developmental speech disorders using data from the Colorado Adoption Project.' *Journal of Speech and Hearing Research 40*, 4, 778–791.

Fenson, L., Dale, P.S., Reznick, J. S., Bates, E., Thal, D. J. and Pethnick, S. (1994) 'Variability in early communicative development.' *Monographs on Social Research and Child Development 59*, 1–173.

Foil, C. R. and Alber, S. R. (2002) 'Fun and effective ways to build your students' vocabulary.' *Intervention in School and Clinic 37*, 3, 131–139.

Fonagy, P. and Target, M. (1997) 'Attachment and reflective function: their role in self-organization.' *Development and Psychopathology 9*, 679–700.

Francis, D. J., Fletcher, J. M., Shaywitz, B. A., Shaywitz, S. E. and Rourke, B. P. (1996) 'Defining learning and language disabilities: conceptual and psychometric issues with the use of IQ tests.' *Language, Speech and Hearing Services in Schools 27*, 2, 132–143.

Freedman, E. and Wiig, E. H. (1995) 'Classroom management and instruction for adolescents with language disabilities.' *Seminars in Speech and Language 16*, 1, 46–64.

Frisk, M. (1999) 'A complex background in children and adolescents with psychiatric disorders: developmental delay, dyslexia, heredity, slow cognitive processing and adverse social factors in a multifactorial entirety.' *European Child and Adolescent Psychiatry 8*, 3, 225–236.

Fristad, M. A., Topolsky, S., Weller, E. B. and Weller, R. A. (1992) 'Depression and learning disabilities in children.' *Journal of Affective Disorders 26*, 53–58.

Fujiki, M., Brinton, B. and Todd, C. M. (1996) 'Social skills of children with specific language impairment.' *Language, Speech and Hearing Services in Schools 27*, 3, 195–202.

Fulk, B. M., Brugham, F. J. and Lohman, D. A. (1998) 'Motivation and self-regulation: a comparison of students with learning and behavioural problems.' *Remedial and Special Education 19*, 5, 300–309.

Gallagher, T. M. (1999) 'Interrelationships among children's language, behaviour, and emotional problems.' *Topics in Language Disorder 19*, 2, 1–15.

Gallico, R. (1986) 'The application of a discrepancy model with a cognitive behaviour profile for differentiating learning disabilities from emotional disturbance.' *Dissertations Abstract International 47*, 5.

Gardner, H. (1983) *Frames of Mind: The Theory of Multiple Intelligences.* New York: Basic Books.

Garland, A. F., Landsverk, J. L., Hough, R. L. and Ellis-Mcleod, E. (1996) 'Type of maltreatment as a predictor of mental health service use for children in foster care.' *Child Abuse and Neglect 20*, 8, 675–688.

Garton, A. F. (1992) *Social Interaction and the Development of Language and Cognition.* Hillsdale, NJ: Lawrence Erlbaum.

Gerber, A. (1993) *Language Related Learning Disabilities: Their Nature and Treatment.* Baltimore, MD: Paul H. Brookes.

Gesten, M., Coster, W., Schneider-Rosen, K., Carlson, V. and Cicchetti, D. (1986) 'The socio-economic bases of communication functioning: quality of attachment, language development and early maltreatment.' In M. E. Lamb, A. L. Brown and B. Rogoff (eds) *Advances in Development Psychology 4.* Hillsdale, NJ: Lawrence Erlbaum.

Giddan, J. J. (1991) 'School children with emotional problems and communication deficits: implications for speech language pathologists.' *Language, Speech and Hearing Services in Schools 22*, 291–295.

Giddan, J. J., Milling, L. and Campbell, N. B. (1996) 'Unrecognised language and speech deficits in preadolescent psychiatric inpatients.' *American Journal of Orthopsychiatry 66*, 1, 291–295.

Gilfix, J. and Heller Kahn, N. (1999) *The Special Playroom: A Young Child's Guide to Play Therapy.* CH175 Child Advocacy. Montana Coalition Against Domestic Violence and Sexual Violence (www.mcadsv.com)

Gillam, R. B. and Carlile, R. M. (1997) 'Oral reading and story retelling of students with specific language impairment.' *Language, Speech and Hearing Services in Schools 28*, 1, 30–42.

Gillam, R. B. and Hoffman, L. M. (2000) 'Information processing and language learning in children with specific language impairment.' In L. Verhoeven and H. van Balkom (eds) *Classification of Developmental Language Disorders: Theoretical Issues and Clinical Implications.* Hove, UK: Lawrence Erlbaum.

Gillam, R. B., Pena, E. D. and Miller, L. (1999) 'Dynamic assessment of narrative and expository discourse.' *Topics in Language Disorders 20*, 1, 33–47.

Gilliam, W. S. and De Mesquita, P. B. (2000) 'The relationship between language and cognitive development and emotional-behavioural problems in financially disadvantaged preschoolers: a longitudinal investigation.' *Early Child Development and Care 162*, 9–24.

Glass, N. (2001) 'What works for children – the political issues.' *Children and Society 15*, 14–20.

Gleason, J. B. (ed) (1997) *The Development of Language,* 4th Edn. Needham Heights, MA: Allyn and Bacon.

Goerge, R. M., Van Voorhis, J., Grant, S., Casey, K. and Robinson, M. (1992) 'Special-educational experiences of foster children: an empirical study.' *Child Welfare 71*, 5, 419–437.

Goodman, R. (1997) 'Child mental health: who is responsible? An overextended remit.' *British Medical Journal 314*, 813–814.

Goodyer, I. M. (2000) 'Language difficulties and psychopathology.' In D. V. M. Bishop and L. B. Leonard (eds) *Speech and Language Impairments in Children: Causes, Characteristics, Intervention and Outcome.* Hove, East Sussex: Psychology Press.

Gray, C. and Jonker, S. (eds) (1994) *The Social Story Book.* Arlington, TX: Future Education.

Greenaway, C. (2000) 'Autism and Asperger's syndrome: strategies to promote prosocial behaviours.' *Educational Psychology in Practice 16*, 4, 469–486.

Greenberg, M. T., Kusche, C. A., Cook, E. T. and Quamma, J. P. (1995) 'Promoting emotional competence in school-aged children: the effects of the PATHS curriculum.' *Development and Psychopathology 7*, 117–136.

Griffiths, F. (2002) *Communication Counts.* London: David Fulton.

Gualtieri, C. T., Koriath, U., Van Bourgondien, M. and Saleeby, N. (1983) 'Language disorders in children referred for psychiatric services.' *Journal of the American Academy of Child Psychiatry 22*, 165–171.

Guralnick, M. J., Connor, R. T., Hammond, M. A., Gottman, J. M. and Kinnish, K. (1995) 'The peer relations of preschool children with communication disorders.' *Journal of Speech and Hearing Research 38*, 2, 446–462.

Haight, W. and Sachs, K. (1995) 'The portrayal of negative emotions during mother–child pretend play.' *Child Development 69*, 33–46.

Halliday, M. (1991) 'The notion of "context" in language education.' In L. Thao and M. McCausland (eds) *Language Education: Interaction and Development. Proceedings of the International Conference, Ho Chi Minh City, Vietnam.* Launceston: University of Tasmania.

Hamil, P. and Boyd, B. (2001) 'Striving for inclusion: evaluation of provision for young people with social, emotional and behavioural difficulties in secondary schools in a Scottish council.' *Scottish Educational Review 33*, 2, 142–156.

Hancock, T. B., Kaiser, A. P. and Delaney, E. M. (2002) 'Teaching parents of preschoolers at high risk: strategies to support language and positive behavior.' *Topics in Early Childhood Special Education 22*, 4, 191–212.

Hart, B. and Risley, T. R. (1995) *Meaningful Differences in the Everyday Experience of Young American Children.* Baltimore, MD: Brookes.

Hayden, C. (1997) 'Exclusion from primary school: children "in need" and children with "special educational need".' *Emotional and Behavioural Difficulties 2*, 3, 36–44.

Hayden, D. A. and Pukonen, M. (1996) 'Language intervention programming for preschool children with social and pragmatic disorders.' In J. M. Beitchman and N. J. Cohen (eds) *Language, Learning, and Behavior Disorders: Developmental, Biological and Clinical Perspectives.* New York: Cambridge University Press.

Haynes, C. and Naidoo, S. (1991) *Children with Specific Speech and Language Impairment.* Oxford: MacKeith Press/Blackwell Scientific.

Headstart (2002) *Making a Difference in the Lives of Infants and Toddlers and Their Families: The Impacts of Early Headstart.* Executive Summary. Administration for Children and Families, U.S. Department of Health and Human Services (www.acf.hhs.gov/programs).

Heath, A. F., Colton, M. and Aldgate, J. (1989) 'The educational progress of children in and out of care.' *British Journal of Social Work 19*, 6, 447–460.

Heath, A. F., Colton, M. J. and Aldgate, J. (1994) 'Failure to escape – a longitudinal study of foster children's educational attainment.' *British Journal of Social Work 24*, 3, 241–260.

Henggeler, S. W., Schoenwald, S. K., Borduin, C. M., Rowland, M. D. and Cunningham, P. B. (1998) *Multisystems Treatment of Antisocial Behaviour in Children and Adolescents.* New York: Guilford Press.

Hesse, P. and Cicchetti, D. (1982) 'Perspectives on an integrated theory of emotional development.' *New Directions for Child Development 16*, 3–48. San Francisco, CA: Jossey-Bass.

HM Inspectors of Schools and the Social Work Services Inspectorate (2001) *Learning with Care: The Education of Children Looked After Away from Home by Local Authorities.* Joint Report.

Horowitz, S. M. (2000) 'Specialized assessments for children in foster care.' *Pediatrics*, July, 106, 1, 59–66.

Horowitz, S. M., Simms, M. D. and Farrington, R. M. (1994) 'The impact of developmental and behavioural problems on the exit of children from foster care.' *Journal of Developmental and Behavioural Pediatrics 15*, 105–110.

Jackson, S. and Martin, P. Y. (1998) 'Surviving the care system: education and resilience.' *Journal of Adolescence 21*, 569–583.

James, A. (2002) 'Container-contained: psychoanalytically informed work in a Social Services unit for disturbed adolescent boys.' *Therapeutic Communities 23*, 3, 192–203.

Jerome, A. C., Fujiki, M., Brinton, B. and James, S. L. (2002) 'Self-esteem in children with specific language impairment.' *Journal of Speech, Language and Hearing Research 45*, 4, 700–714.

Joffe, B. S., Doyle, J. and Penn, C. (1996) 'The persisting communication difficulties of "remediated" language impaired children.' *European Journal of Disorders of Communication 31*, 369.

Johnson, M. (1996) *Functional Language in the Classroom.* Manchester: Manchester Metropolitan University (Department of Psychology and Speech Pathology).

Johnston, S. and Reichle, J. (1993) 'Designing and implementing interventions to decrease challenging behaviour.' *Language, Speech and Hearing Services in Schools 24*, 225–235.

Jones, D. and Ramchandani, P. (1999) *Child Sexual Abuse: Informing Practice from Research.* Abingdon: Radcliffe Medical Press.

Jones, J. (1996) 'Speech and language therapy in child psychiatry.' In R. Chesson and D. Chisolm (eds) *Child Guidance Units at the Crossroads.* London: Jessica Kingsley Publishers.

Jones, J. and Chesson, R. (2000) 'Falling through the screen.' *Royal College of Speech and Language Therapists Bulletin 579*, July, 8–9.

Kaiser, A. P., Hancock, T. B., Cai, X., Foster, E. M. and Hester, P. P. (2000) 'Parent-reported behavioural problems and language delays in boys and girls enrolled in Headstart classrooms.' *Behavioural Disorders 22*, 117–130.

Kaiser, A. P., Hemmeter, M. L., Ostrovsky, M. M., Fischer, R., Yoder, P. and Keefer, M. (1996) 'The effects of teaching parents to use responsive interaction strategies.' *Topics in Early Childhood Special Education 16*, 3, 375–406.

Kaler, S. R. and Kopp, C. (1990) 'Compliance and comprehension in very young toddlers.' *Child Development 61*, 1997–2003.

Kendall, P. C. and Braswell, L. (1985) *Cognitive-behavioural Therapy for Impulsive Children.* New York: Guilford Press.

Kim, O. H. (1999) 'Language characteristics and social skills of children with Attention Deficit Hyperactivity Disorder.' *Dissertation Abstracts International, The Humanities and Social Sciences 60*, 5, 1513–1550.

Knutson, J. F. and Sullivan, P. M. (1993) 'Communicative disorders as a risk factor in abuse.' *Topics in Language Disorders 13*, 4, 1–14.

Kopp, C. B. (1989) 'Regulation of distress and negative emotions: a developmental view.' *Developmental Psychology 25*, 343–354.

Kotsopoulos, A. and Boodoosingh, L. (1987) 'Language and speech disorders in children attending a day psychiatric programme.' *British Journal of Disorders of Communication 22*, 227–236.

Kusche, C., Cook, E. and Greenberg, M. (1993) 'Neuropsychology and cognitive functioning in children with anxiety: externalising and comorbid psychopathology.' *Journal of Clinical Child Psychology 22*, 172–195.

Lahey, M. (1990) 'Who shall be called language disordered? Some reflections and one perspective.' *Journal of Speech and Hearing Disorders 55*, 612–620.

Laplante, D. P., Zelazo, P. R. and Kearsley, R. B. (1991) 'The effect of a short-term parent implemented treatment programme on the production of expressive language.' *Society for Research in Child Development Abstracts 8*, 336.

Law, J. and Conway, J. (1989) *Child Abuse and Neglect: The Effect on Communication Development. A Review of the Literature.* London: Afasic.

Law, J. and Sivyer, S. (2003) 'Promoting the communication skills of primary school children excluded from school or at risk of exclusion: an intervention study.' *Child Language Teaching and Therapy 19*, 1, 1–27.

Law, J., Boyle, J., Harris, F., Harkness, A. and Nye, C. (1998) 'Screening for speech and language delay: a systematic review of the literature.' *International Journal of Language and Communication Disorders 33*, suppl. 21–23.

Law, J., Boyle, J., Harris, F., Harkness, A. and Nye, C. (2000a) 'Prevalence and natural history of primary speech and language delay: findings from a systematic review of the literature.' *International Journal of Language and Communication Disorders 35*, 2, 165–189.

Law, J., Lindsay, G., Peacey, N., Gascoigne, M., Solof, N., Radford, J., Band, S. and Fitzgerald, L. (2000b) *Provision for Children with Speech and Language Needs in England and Wales: Facilitating Communication Between Education and Health Services.* London: DFEE DOH.

Leahy, M. and Dodd, B. (2002) 'Why should secondary schools come second?' *Royal College of Speech and Language Therapists Bulletin*, May, 601.

Lee, F. and Wright, J. (2001) 'Developing an emotional awareness programme for pupils with moderate learning difficulties at Durants School.' *Emotional and Behavioural Difficulties 6*, 3, 186–199.

Leonard, L. (1998) *Children with Specific Language Impairment* (Language Speech and Communication series). Cambridge, MA: MIT Press.

Lesser, G., Fifer, G. and Clark, D. (1965) 'Mental abilities of children from different social class and cultural groups.' *Monographs of the Society for Research in Child Development 30*, 1–15.

Lewis, B. A., Cox, N. J. and Bynard, P. J. (1993) 'Segregation analysis of speech and language disorders.' *Behavioural Genetics 23*, 2391–2397.

Licht, B. G. (1992) 'Achievement related beliefs in children with learning disabilities: impact on motivation and strategic learning.' In L. Meltzer (ed) *Strategy Assessment and Training for Students with Learning Disabilities: From Theory to Practice.* Austin, TX: Pro-Ed.

Lloyd, M. E. and Hilliard, A. M. (1989) 'Accuracy of self recording as a function of repeated experience with different self-control contingencies.' *Child and Family Behaviour Therapy 11*, 2, 1–14.

Local Government Management Board (1997) *Social Services Workforce Analysis Main Report.* 1997 Survey (www.lgmb.gov.uk/).

Loftus, E. and Hoffman, H. G. (1989) 'Misinformation and memory: the creation of new memories.' *Journal of Experimental Psychology 118*, 100–104.

Loucks, Y. and Gallagher, T. (1988) 'Dispute initiations among SLI and normal language pre-schoolers.' Paper presented at the American Speech-Language-Hearing Association Convention, November, St Louis, MO.

Love, A. J. and Thompson, M. G. G. (1988) 'Language disorders and attention deficit disorders in young children referred for psychiatric services: analysis of prevalence and a conceptual synthesis.' *Journal of Orthopsychiatry 58*, 811–816.

Lynham, D. R. and Henry, B. (2001) 'The role of neuropsychological deficits in conduct disorders.' In J. Hill and B. Maughan (eds) *Conduct Disorders in Childhood and Adolescence.* Cambridge: Child and Adolescent Psychiatry.

MacGregor, R., Pullar, A. and Cundall, D. (1994) 'Silent at school – elective mutism and abuse.' *Archives of Disease in Childhood 70*, 540–541.

McCann, J. B., James, A., Wilson, S. and Dunn, G. (1996) 'Prevalence of psychiatric disorders in young people in the care system.' *British Medical Journal 313*, 1529–1530.

McCartney, E. (ed) (1999) *Speech/Language Therapists and Teachers Working Together: A Systems Approach to Collaboration.* London: Whurr Publishers.

McCauley, R. J. (1996) 'Familiar strangers: criterion-referenced measures in communication disorders.' *Language, Speech, and Hearing Services in Schools 27*, 2, 122–131.

McCauley, R. J. and Swisher, L. (1987) 'Are maltreated children at risk for speech or language impairment? An unanswered question.' *Journal of Speech and Hearing Disorders 52*, 301–302.

McDonough, K. M. (1989) 'Analysis of the expressive language characteristics of emotionally handicapped students in social interactions.' *Behavioural Disorders 14*, 127–139.

McDonough, S. (1993) 'Interaction guidance: understanding and treating early infant–caregiver relationship disturbances.' In C. Zeanah (ed) *The Handbook of Infant Mental Health.* New York: Guilford Press.

McGee, R., Williams, S., Share, D. L., Anderson, J. and Silva, P. A. (1986) 'The relationship between specific reading retardation, general reading backwardness and behavioural problems in a large sample of Dunedin boys: a longitudinal study from five to eleven years.' *Journal of Child Psychology and Psychiatry 27*, 5, 507–610.

McIntyre, A. and Keesler, T. Y. (1986) 'Psychological disorders among foster children.' *Journal of Child Psychology 15*, 297–303.

Manolson, A. (1992) *It Takes Two to Talk*, 2nd Edn. Toronto: Hanen Early Language Resource Centre.

Martin-Devins, M. T. (2001) 'A collaborative approach to addressing the language needs of adolescents with school-based difficulties.' Paper presented at the IASLT and TCD National Conference, Dublin, Ireland.

Masten, A. and Coatsworth, D. (1998) 'Development of competence in favourable and unfavourable environments: A tale of resources risk and resilience.' *American Psychologist 53*, 205–220.

Mathieson, B., Skuse, D., Wolke, D. and Reilly, S. (1989) 'Oral-motor dysfunction and failure to thrive among inner city infants.' *Developmental Medicine and Child Neurology 31*, 293–302.

Mayer, J. D. and Salovey, P. (1997) 'What is emotional intelligence?' In P. Salovey and D. Sluyter (eds) *Emotional Development and Emotional Intelligence: Educational Implications.* New York: Basic Books.

Meltzer, H., Gatward, R., Goodman, R. and Ford, T. (2000) *The Mental Health of Children and Adolescents in Great Britain.* Summary report. London: The Office for National Statistics.

Meltzer, L. (1992) *Strategy Assessment and Training for Students with Learning Disabilities: From Theory to Practise.* Austin, TX: Pro-Ed.

Menyuk, P. (1977) *Language and Maturation.* Cambridge, MA: MIT Press.

Merrell, A. W. and Plante, E. (1997) 'Norm-referenced test interpretation in the diagnostic process.' *Language, Speech and Hearing Services in Schools 28*, 50–58.

Moffit, T. E. and Lynham, D. R. (1994) 'The neuropsychology of conduct disorder and delinquency: implications for understanding antisocial behaviour.' In D. Fowles, P. Stuker and S. Goodman (eds) *Psychopathology and Antisocial Personality: A Developmental Perspective.* New York: Springer.

Moffit, T. E., Caspi, A., Dickson, N., Silva, P. and Stanton, W. (1996) 'Childhood-onset versus adolescent-onset antisocial conduct problems in males: natural history from ages 3–18.' *Development and Psychology 8*, 399–424.

Montgomery, J. W. (1995) 'Sentence comprehension in children with SLI: the role of phonological working memory.' *Journal of Speech and Hearing Research 38*, 187–199.

Morris, J. T. (1996) 'Excluded pupils – the mismatch between the problem and solutions.' *Emotional and Behavioural Difficulties 1*, 35–38.

Mosley, J. (1996) *Quality Circle Time in the Primary Classroom.* Cambridge: LDA.

Muir, N. (1997) 'Semantic pragmatic disorder and the role of the speech and language therapist in psychiatry.' In J. France and N. Muir (eds) *Communication and the Mentally Ill Patient: Developmental and Linguistic Approaches to Schizophrenia.* London: Jessica Kingsley Publishers.

168 CHILDREN WITH EBD AND COMMUNICATION PROBLEMS

Mukaddes, N. M., Bilge, S., Alyanak, B. and Kora, M. E. (2000) 'Clinical characteristics and treatment responses in cases diagnosed as reactive attachment disorder.' *Child Psychiatry and Human Development 30*, 4, 273–287.

Myer, C. M. and Fitton, C. M. (1988) 'Vocal cord paralysis following child abuse.' *International Journal of Pediatric Otorhinolaryngology 15*, 217–220.

Naremore, R. C., Densmore, A. E. and Harman, D. R. (1995) *Language Intervention with School-aged Children: Conversation, Narrative and Text.* San Diego, CA: Singular Publishing Group.

Nathan, L., Stackhouse, J. and Goulandris, N. (1998) 'Speech processing abilities in children with speech vs. speech and language difficulties.' *International Journal of Language and Communication Disorders Supplement 33*, 457–462.

Nelson, N. W. (1989) 'Curriculum-based language assessment and intervention.' *Language, Speech and Hearing Services in Schools 20*, 170–184.

Nippold, M. A. (1993) 'Clinical forum: adolescent language developmental markers in adolescent language: syntax, semantics and pragmatics.' *Language, Speech and Hearing Services in Schools 24*, 21–28.

Novick, R. (1998) 'The comfort corner: fostering resiliency and emotional intelligence.' *Childhood Education 74*, 4, 200–204.

Office for Standards in Education (Ofsted) (1999) *Principles into Practice: Effective Education for Pupils with Emotional and Behavioural Difficulties.* London: HMSO. www.ofsted.gov.uk

Office for Standards in Education (Ofsted) (2001) *Raising the Achievement of Children in Public Care.* London: HMSO. www.ofsted.gov.uk

Osofsky, J., Cohen, G. and Drell, M. (1995) 'The effects of trauma in young children: a case of 2-year-old twins.' *International Journal of Psychoanalysis 76*, 595–607.

Papaeliou, C., Minadakis, G. and Cavouras, D. (2002) 'Acoustic patterns of infant vocalisations expressing emotions and communicative functions.' *Journal of Speech, Language and Hearing Research 45*, 2, 311–317.

Parsons, C. (1994) *Excluding Primary School Children.* London: Family Policy Studies Centre.

Patnaik, B. and Babu, N. (2001) 'Relationship between children's acquisition of a theory of mind and their understanding of mental terms.' *Psycho-Lingua 31*, 1, 3–8.

Paul, R. and James, D. F. (1990) 'Language delay and parental perceptions (Letter to the editor).' *Journal of the American Academy of Child and Adolescent Psychiatry 29*, 669–670.

Paulger, B. (1999) 'Therapy for real life.' *Speech and Language Therapy in Practice*, Summer, 12–14.

Peck, D. (2002) 'What's the problem? A guide to running a problem-solving workshop for parents/carers of children with language and communication difficulties.' *Support for Learning 17*, 1, 39–43.

Perry, B. D., Pollard, R. A., Blakley, T. L., Baker, W. L. and Vigilante, D. (1995) 'Childhood trauma, the neurobiology of adaptation, and "use-dependent" development of the brain: how "states" become "traits".' *Infant Mental Health Journal 16*, 4, 271–291.

Pickstone, C. (2003) 'A pilot study of paraprofessional screening of child language in community settings.' *Child Language Teaching and Therapy 19*, 1, 49–65.

Pollak, S. D., Cicchetti, D., Hornung, K. and Reed, A. (2000) 'Recognizing emotion in faces: developmental effects of child abuse and neglect.' *Developmental Psychology 36*, 5, 679–688.

Prizant, B. M., Audet, L. R., Burke, G. M., Hummel, L. J., Maher, S. R. and Theadore, G. (1990) 'Communication disorders and emotional/behavioural disorders in children and adolescents.' *Journal of Speech and Hearing Disorders 55*, 179–192.

Rapin, I. (1996) 'Practitioner review: developmental language disorders: a clinical update.' *Journal of Child Psychology and Psychiatry 37*, 643–655.

Rauch, S. L., van der Kolk, B. A., Fisler, R. E., Alpert, N. M., Orr, S. P., Savage, C. R., Fischman, A. J., Jenike, M. A. and Pitman, R. K. (1996) 'A symptom provocation study of post-traumatic stress disorder using positron emission tomography and script driven imagery.' *Archives of General Psychiatry 53*, 380–387.

Redmond, S. M. and Rice, M. L. (1998) 'The socioemotional behaviors of children with SLI: social adaptation or social deviance?' *Journal of Speech, Language and Hearing Research 41*, 688–700.

Rende, R. D., Plomin, R., Reiss, D. and Hetherington, E. M. (1993) 'Genetic and environmental influences on depressive symptomatology in adolescence: individual differences and extreme scores.' *Journal of Child Psychology and Psychiatry 34*, 1387–1398.

Rhodes, J. and Ajmal, Y. (1995) *Solution Focused Thinking in Schools.* London: BT Press.

Rice, M. (1993) 'Don't talk to him: he's weird; a social consequences account of language and social interactions.' In A. P. Kaiser and D. B. Gray (eds) *Enhancing Children's Communication: Research Foundations for Intervention.* Baltimore, MD: Brookes.

Rice, M. L., Wexler, K. and Hershberger, S. (1998) 'Tense over time: the longitudinal course of tense acquisition in children with specific language impairment.' *Journal of Speech, Language and Hearing Research 41*, 6, 1412–1431.

Rice, M. L., Wilcox, K. and Hadley, P. (1992) 'The role of language and social skills.' In F. L. Parker *et al.* (eds) *The Social Use of Language: Research Foundations for Early Language Interventions.* Baltimore, MD: Brookes.

Rinaldi, W. (1992) *The Social Use of Language Programme: Enhancing the Social Communication Skills of Children and Teenagers with Special Educational Needs.* Windsor: NFER Nelson.

Rinaldi, W. (1996) 'The inner life of youngsters with specific developmental language disorder.' In V. P. Varma (ed) *The Inner Life of Children with Special Needs.* London: Whurr Publishers.

Risley-Curtiss, C., Combs-Orme, T., Chernoff, R. and Heisler, A. (1996) 'Health care utilisation by children entering foster care.' *Research on Social Work Practice 6*, 4, 442–461.

Rissman, A. S., Curtiss, S. and Tallal, P. (1990) 'School placement outcomes of young language impaired children.' *Journal of Speech Language Pathology and Audiology 14*, 49–58.

Robinson, J. L. and Acevedo, M. C. (2001) 'Infant reactivity and reliance on mother during emotion challenges: prediction of cognition and language skills in a low-income sample.' *Child Development 72*, 2, 402–415.

Rock, E. E., Fessler, M. and Church, R. P. (1997) 'The concomitance of learning disabilities and emotional/behavioural disorders: a conceptual model.' *Journal of Learning Disabilities 30*, 3, 245–263.

Rosenthal, S. L. and Simeonsson, R. J. (1991) 'Communication skills in emotionally disturbed and nondisturbed adolescents.' *Behavioral Disorders 16*, 192–199.

Roy, P., Rutter, M. and Pickles, A. (2000) 'Institutional care: risk from family background or pattern of rearing?' *Journal of Child Psychology, Psychiatry and Allied Disciplines 41*, 2, 11.

Ruff, H. A., Blank, S. and Barnett, H. L. (1990) 'Early intervention in the context of foster care.' *Journal of Developmental and Behavioural Pediatrics 11*, 265–268.

Russell, R. L., Greenwald, S. and Shirk, S. R. (1991) 'Language change in child psychotherapy: a meta-analytical review.' *Journal of Clinical and Consulting Psychology 59*, 916–919.

Russell, S. C. and Sternberg, L. (1997) 'Psychoeducational problems that present as academic difficulties.' *Child and Adolescent Psychiatric Clinics of North America 6*, 3, 489–508.

Rutter, M. and Mawhood, L. (1991) 'The long term sequelae of specific development disorders of speech and language.' In M. Rutter and P. Casaer (eds) *Biological Risk Factors for Psychosocial Disorders.* Cambridge: Cambridge University Press.

Saarni, C. (1997) 'Emotional competence and self regulation in childhood.' In P. Salovey and D. Sluyter (eds) *Emotional Development and Emotional Intelligence: Educational Implications.* New York: Basic Books.

Sachs, J., Brown, R. and Salerno, R. (1976) 'Adult's speech to children.' In W. von Raffler Engler and Y. Lebrun (eds) *Baby Talk and Infant Speech.* Lisse: Peter de Riddler Press.

Sage, R. (2000) *Class Talk.* Stafford: Network Educational Press.

Sage, R. (2002) 'Start talking and stop misbehaving: teaching pupils to communicate, think and act appropriately.' *Emotional and Behavioural Difficulties 7*, 2, 85–96.

Salovey, P. and Sluyter, D. (eds) (1997) *Emotional Development and Emotional Intelligence: Educational Implications.* New York: Basic Books.

Sanger, D., Maag, J. W. and Shapera, N. R. (1994) 'Language problems among students with emotional and behavioral disorders.' *Intervention in School and Clinic 30*, 2, 103–108.

Sattler, J. M., Feldman, J. and Bonahan, A. L. (1985) 'Parental estimates of children's receptive vocabulary.' *Psychology in the Schools 22*, 303–307.

Sawyer, R. J. and Dubowitz, H. (1994) 'School performance of children in kinship care.' *Child Abuse and Neglect 18*, 7, 587–597.

Schaffer, R. (1989) 'Early social development.' In A. Slater and G. Bremner (eds) *Infant Development.* London: Lawrence Erlbaum.

Schneiderman, M., Connors, M. M., Fribourg, A., Gries, L. and Gonzales, M. (1998) 'Mental health services for children in out-of-home care.' *Child Welfare 77*, 1, 29–40.

Schultheis, A. M. M. (2001) 'Language needs of preschoolers with behavior problems.' *Dissertation Abstracts International Section A: Humanities and Social Sciences 61*, 12A, 4734.

Scott, C. M. (1988) 'Producing complex sentences.' *Topics in Language Disorders 8*, 2, 44–62.

Secord, W. A. and Wiig, E. H. (1992) *Developing a Collaborative Language Intervention Programme.* Buffalo, NY: EDUCOM Associates.

Shapiro, T. and Kalogerakis, A. (1997) 'Adolescent language and music.' In J. D. Noshpitz (ed) *Handbook of Child and Adolescent Psychiatry.* New York: Wiley.

Sheilds, J., Varley, R., Broks, P. and Simpson, A. (1996) 'Hemispheric function in developmental language disorders and high level autism.' *Developmental Medicine and Child Neurology 38*, 473–486.

Siegel, L. S. and Ryan, E. B. (1989) 'The development of working memory in normally achieving and subtypes of learning disabled children.' *Child Development 60*, 973–980.

Sigafoos, J. (2000) 'Communication development and aberrant behavior in children with developmental disabilities.' *Education and Training in Mental Retardation and Developmental Disabilities 35*, 2, 168–176.

Sigman, M. and Capps, L. (1997) *Children with Autism: A Developmental Perspective.* Cambridge, MA: Harvard University Press.

Silva, P. A., Justin, C., McGee, R. and Williams, S. (1984) 'Some developmental and behavioural characteristics of seven-year-old children.' *British Journal of Disorders of Communication 19*, 107–154.

Silva, P. A., Williams, S. and McGee, R. (1987) 'A longitudinal study of children with developmental language delay at age three: later intelligence, reading and behaviour problems.' *Developmental Medicine and Child Neurology 29*, 630–640.

Simms, M. D. and Halfon, N. (1994) 'The health care needs of children in foster care: a research agenda.' *Child Welfare 73*, 5, 505–520.

Singer, V. A. (2000) 'Improved language skills as a by-product of parent–child interaction therapy with behavior problem children at risk for childhood physical abuse.' *Dissertation Abstracts International: Section B: The Sciences and Engineering 60*, 12B, 6384.

Snow, C. E. (1986) 'Conversations with children.' In P. Fletcher and M. Garman (eds) *Language Acquisition*, 2nd Edn. Cambridge: Cambridge University Press.

Snow, C. (1998) 'Understanding the nature of language development.' Presented at the Denny Cantwell Institute on Language and Child Psychiatry, Annual Meeting of the American Academy of Child and Adolescent Psychiatry, Anaheim, CA.

Snyder-McLean, L., Solomonson, B., McLean, J. and Sack, S. (1984) 'Structuring joint action routines: a strategy for facilitating communication and language development in the classroom.' *Seminars in Speech and Language 5*, 213–228.

Stacey, K. (1995) 'Language as an exclusive or inclusive concept: reaching beyond the verbal.' *Australian and New Zealand Journal of Family Therapy 16*, 3, 123–132.

Stark, R. and Tallal, P. (1981) 'Selection of children with specific language deficits.' *Journal of Speech and Hearing Disorders 6*, 114–122.

Stark, R. E. and Tallal, P. (1988) *Language, Speech and Reading Disorders in Children: Neuropsychological Studies.* Boston, MA: A College-Hill Publication.

Stothard, S. E., Snowling, M. J., Bishop, D. V. M., Chipchase, B. B. and Caplan, C. A. (1998) 'Language impaired pre-schoolers: a follow-up into adolescence.' *Journal of Speech, Language and Hearing Research 41*, 407–418.

Sure Start (2002) *Supporting Families who have Children with Special Needs and Disabilities.* London: DfES Publications.

Swartzlander, P. and Naremore, R. (1989) 'Stories and scripts: performance of normal and language delayed preschoolers.' Paper presented at the American Speech-Language-Hearing Convention, Atlanta, GA.

Swinson, J. and Cording, M. (2002) 'Assertive discipline in an EBD school.' *British Journal of Special Education 29*, 3, 72–75.

Swinson, J. and Melling, R. (1995) 'Assertive discipline: four wheels on this wagon – a reply to Robinson and Mains.' *Educational Psychology in Practice 11*, 30, 1–8.

Swinson, J., Woof, C. and Melling, R. (2003) 'Including emotional and behavioural difficulties pupils in a mainstream comprehensive: a study of the behaviour of pupils and classes.' *Educational Psychology in Practice 19*, 1, 66–75.

Tallal, P. (1988) 'Developmental language disorders.' In J. F. Kavanaugh and T. J. Truss (eds) *Learning Disabilities: Proceedings of the National Conference.* Parkton, MD: York Press.

Tamis-Lemonda, C. and Bornstein, M. (1989) 'Habituation and maternal encouragement of attention in infancy as predictors of toddler language, play and representational competence.' *Child Development 50*, 738–751.

Tannock, R. and Schachar, R. (1996) 'Executive dysfunction as an underlying mechanism of behaviour and language problems in attention deficit hyperactivity disorder.' In J. M. Beitchman and N. J. Cohen (eds) *Language, Learning and Behaviour Disorders: Developmental, Biological and Clinical Perspectives.* New York: Cambridge University Press.

Tannock, R., Purvis, K. L. and Schachar, R. J. (1993) 'Narrative abilities in children with Attention Deficit Hyperactivity Disorder and normal peers.' *Journal of Abnormal Child Psychology 21*, 103–117.

Teale, S. (2000) *Rainbows of Intelligence: Exploring How Students Learn.* California: Corwin/Sage.

Thomas, C. C., Corea, V. I. and Morsink, C. V. (1995) *Interactive Teaming: Consultation and Collaboration in Special Programmes*, 2nd Edn. Englewood Cliffs, NJ: Merrill.

Thompson, A. H. and Fuhr, D. (1992) 'Emotional disturbance in fifty children in the care of a child welfare system.' *Journal of Social Service Research 15*, 95–112.

Tomblin, J. B. (1983) 'An examination of the concept of disorder in the study of language variation.' *Proceedings from the Fourth Wisconsin Symposium on Research on Child Language Disorders* (pp.81–109). Madison, WI: University of Wisconsin.

Tomblin, J. B., Records, N., Buckwalter, P., Zhang, X., Smith, E. and O'Brien, M. (1997) 'Prevalence of specific language impairment in kindergarten children.' *Journal of Speech, Language and Hearing Research 40*, 6, 12–45.

Toppelberg, C. O. (2000) 'Language disorders: a 10-year research update review.' *Journal of the American Academy of Child and Adolescent Psychiatry 39*, 2, 143–152.

Training Organisation for the Personal and Social Services (1999) *The National Training Organisation for Social Care.* Supplementary Report on Child Care. London: TOPSS.

Trapp, E. P. and Evan, J. (1960) 'Functional articulatory defect and performance in nonverbal tasks.' *Journal of Speech and Hearing Disorders 25*, 176–180.

Trenerry, M. (1998) 'Managing learner self-image as a means of effecting reading progress in primary school children with entrenched reading difficulties.' Unpublished M.Ed dissertation, University of Plymouth.

Urquiza, A. J., Wirth, S. J., Petersen, M. S. and Singer, V. A. (1994) 'Screening and evaluating abused and neglected children entering protective custody.' *Child Welfare 73*, 155–171.

Utting, Sir W. (1997) *People Like Us – The Report of the Review of the Safeguards for Children Living Away from Home.* London: Department of Health/The Welsh Office/The Stationery Office.

Vallance, D. D., Im, N. and Cohen, N. (1999) 'Discourse deficits associated with psychiatric disorders and with language impairments in children.' *Journal of Child Psychology and Psychiatry 40*, 5, 693–704.

Visser, J. (2002) 'The David Wills Lecture 2001. Eternal verities: the strongest links.' *Emotional and Behavioural Difficulties 7*, 2, 68–84.

Visser, J. and Cole, T. (1996) 'An overview of English special school provision for children with emotional and behavioural difficulties.' *Emotional and Behavioural Difficulties 1*, 3, 11–16.

Vygotsky, L. S. (1962) *Thought and Language.* Cambridge, MA: MIT Press.

Ward, L. (1997) *Seen and Heard: Involving Disabled Children and Young People in Research and Development Projects.* York: Joseph Rowntree Foundation.

Weiss, S. (2002) 'How teachers' autobiographies influence their responses to children's behaviours.' *Emotional and Behavioural Difficulties 7*, 2, 109–127.

Wells, C. G. and Robinson, W. P. (1982) 'The role of adult speech in language development.' In C. Fraser and K. Scherer (eds) *The Social Psychology of Language.* Cambridge: Cambridge University Press.

Wells, G. (1981) 'Language, literacy and education.' In G. Wells (ed) *Learning Through Interaction.* Cambridge: Cambridge University Press.

Wells, G. (1986) *Language Development in the Pre-school Years.* Cambridge: Cambridge University Press.

Werner, E. and Smith, R. (1992) *Overcoming the Odds: High Risk Children from Birth to Adulthood.* Ithica, NY: Cornell University Press.

Wetherby, A. and Prizant, B. (1992) 'Profiling young children's communicative competence.' In S. Warren and J. Reichle (eds) *Causes and Effects in Language Disorders and Interventions.* Baltimore: Paul H. Brookes.

White, R. and Benedict, M. (1986) *Health Status and Utilization Patterns of Children in Foster Care: Executive Summary.* Washington, DC: US Department of Health and Human Services, Administration for Children, Youth and Families.

Whitehurst, G. J. and Fischel, J. E. (1994) 'Practitioner review: early developmental language delay: what, if anything, should the clinician do about it?' *Journal of Child Psychology and Psychiatry 35*, 4, 613–648.

Whitman, S. (1996) 'A case study in word finding.' *Child Language Teaching and Therapy 12*, 3, 300–313.

Whitwell, J. (2002) 'Therapeutic child care.' In K. J. White (ed) *NCVCCO Annual Review, Journal 3: Reframing Children's Services.* London: NCVCCO, 94–120.

Wiig, E. H. (1992) 'Strategy training for people with language-learning disabilities.' In L. Meltzer (ed) *Strategy Assessment and Training for Students with Learning Disabilities: From Theory to Practice.* Austin, TX: Pro-Ed.

Wiig, E. H. (1995) 'Assessment of adolescent language.' *Seminars in Speech and Language 16*, 1, 14–31.

Wiig, E. H. and Secord, W. A. (1992) *Test of Word Knowledge.* San Antonio, TX: Psychological Corporation.

Williams, J. P. (1993) 'Comprehension of students with and without learning disabilities: identification of narrative themes and idiosyncratic text representations.' *Journal of Educational Psychology 30*, 509–514.

World Health Organisation (1994) *Classification of Mental and Behavioural Disorders: Diagnostic Criteria for Research* (ICD-10). Geneva: WHO.

Subject Index

173

Author Index